MW01043363

Getting the Gospel Right

Among Other Books by the Author

Before the Face of God, 4 vols.
Choosing My Religion
Chosen by God
Doubt and Assurance
Faith Alone
The Glory of Christ
Grace Unknown
The Holiness of God
The Invisible Hand
Knowing Scripture
The Last Days according to Jesus
Lifeviews
The Mystery of the Holy Spirit
Not a Chance
Now, That's a Good Question!
Pleasing God
Renewing Your Mind
The Soul's Quest for God
Surprised by Suffering
Ultimate Issues
Willing to Believe

Getting the Gospel Right

The Tie That Binds Evangelicals Together

R. C. Sproul

BakerBooks
A Division of Baker Book House Co
Grand Rapids, Michigan 49516

Published by Baker Books
a division of Baker Book House Company
P.O. Box 6287, Grand Rapids, MI 49516-6287

Printed in the United States of America

Library of Congress Cataloging-in-Publication Data is on file at the Library of Congress, Washington, D.C.

ISBN 0-8010-1188-4

For information about Ligonier Ministries and the teaching ministry of R. C. Sproul, visit Ligonier's web site:
http://www.gospelcom.net/ligonier

For information about all releases from Baker Book House, visit our web site:
http://www.bakerbooks.com

Contents

Illustrations

Figures

Tables

Preface

It is axiomatic that a house divided against itself cannot stand. Perhaps the oldest stratagem for military success is the ploy that seeks to "divide and conquer."

When Christians sing together "Blest Be the Tie That Binds," it is not a vacuous exercise in maudlin celebration. The unity Christians share together is so precious that it truly does incarnate the blessing of God to us. This unity is as important as it is at times precarious. By this unity we are strengthened and mutually encouraged to fidelity to Christ and the mission he has given his church.

The loss of Christian unity at any point is tragic and destructive. When that loss threatens our unity in the gospel itself, it is catastrophic. To work toward unity in the gospel is not a matter of ecclesiastical politics; it is a matter that touches the soul of the church itself and the souls of all its members.

To seek unity in the gospel is neither a quixotic crusade nor a frivolous search; it is a matter of the most urgent priority for the Christian. All who embrace the gospel and love its content are visited by a divine mandate to preserve that unity and to defend it together. The gospel is our hope and our life, the most excellent and sweet truth that we have. Beside it lesser theological differences pale into insignificance. In the gospel we experience the power of God unto salvation and hear not only "good news," but the best of all possible news. This unity is so priceless that it is worth contending, fighting, and dying for. It is a family matter for the people of God who have been adopted into the Father's house and who are loyal to the Son, who is our Elder Brother.

The truth of the gospel must be maintained for Christ's sake and for our own. Indeed it is our eternal link to Christ and the means through which we become his in the first place. In the gospel we meet the one who is our only hope in life and death, and by the gospel we acquire a hope that will never leave us ashamed.

For the past few years I have been deeply concerned about the state of evangelical unity in the United States. This concern was provoked initially by the release of the document entitled *Evangelicals and Catholics Together* (ECT)[1] and by the subsequent document entitled *The Gift of Salvation* (GOS).[2] Many Evangelicals were sharply divided by these documents. The effort to seek unity and accord with Roman Catholics had the negative effect of driving a wedge between Evangelicals who formerly were closely allied.

I am numbered among those who believe that both ECT and GOS are seriously flawed. In part 2 of this volume I point out where I think GOS is seriously flawed. But despite the tensions arising from these issues, or because of them, recent months have seen deep discussions among Evangelicals who are seeking to heal the rift engendered by this debate and to come together with a strong and unambiguous declaration of our abiding unity in the gospel, despite our differences over ECT and GOS. In February 1998 discussions took place among those who supported GOS and those who rejected it. These discussions included initially Charles Colson, Timothy George, John Woodbridge, John Ankerberg, Michael Horton, John Armstrong, and myself. We all agreed that what was urgently needed to restore evangelical unity was a joint statement regarding the gospel and justification by faith alone that could reaffirm the unity that has existed historically among a wide and diverse body of evangelical Christians.

As a result of these discussions, a committee was selected to draft a document for the endorsement of evangelical leaders that would cross denominational and sectarian lines. The drafting committee included the following members: John Ankerberg, John Armstrong, John N. Akers, David Neff, Timothy George, J. I. Packer, Erwin Lutzer, John Woodbridge, R. C. Sproul, D. A. Carson, Thomas C. Oden, Scott Hafemann, Keith Davy, Maxie Dunnam, and Harold Myra. Significant input was also given by David Wells.

The drafting committee worked carefully through several drafts and emendations to produce the document that will be analyzed in part 3 of this book, *The Gospel of Jesus Christ: An Evangelical Celebration.*[3] The experience was one marked by a profound spirit of congeniality and mutual respect. The agreements set forth were genuine and heartfelt, leaving the committee members with a spirit of joy and encouragement.

The document was then presented to some prominent evangelical leaders for their endorsement.

Part 1

Controversy Concerning the Gospel

1

Unity and the Gospel

"I believe in the communion of the saints. . . ." This affirmation is declared weekly by myriads of Christians assembled for worship in congregations around the world. It is a crucial affirmation of the Apostles' Creed. That the *communio sanctorum* is an article of catholic Christianity, a universal article of historic Christian faith, underlines the gravity of its importance to the people of God.

This confession has several important aspects to it. Among these is the recognition that Christians from every tribe and tongue and nation, from varied and diverse ecclesiastical communities, enjoy a unity of fellowship that is supernatural in its cause and in the reality of its very essence. A com-union is a union *with* something. In this case it is a union with people. The specific people in view in the creedal affirmation are called "the saints." The reference to "saints" is not restricted to those few extraordinary Christians who have been canonized by a specific institution or who have the title "saint" before their names, such as St. Paul, St. Peter, St. Augustine, St. Francis, and St. Thomas Aquinas. Here the term *saint* is applied to all believers, following the nomenclature of the New Testament, in which rank-and-file Christians are addressed as "saints" or "the holy ones" *(hagioi)*.

Those who are called saints in the New Testament are not so-named because they have achieved a singularly high level of righteousness or a unique degree of sanctification. They are called saints because they have been "set apart" or consecrated to a holy mission and belong to a holy fellowship by virtue of their inclusion in the body of Christ. They are the people who have been regenerated and indwelt by the Holy Spirit. In a word, they are the elect of God from every nation.

The Visible and Invisible Church

The distinction between the visible and invisible church of Christ owes much of its definition to the thinking of St. Augustine, bishop of Hippo in North Africa, who is generally regarded as the greatest theologian of the first millennium of Christian history, if not of all time. Augustine sought to expound the teaching of Christ and his apostles regarding the biblical metaphor of tares and wheat who coexist in the visible or outward congregations of Christian churches. The Bible clearly indicates that it is possible for people to make a profession of faith and unite themselves to a congregation while not actually possessing the faith they profess. Christ spoke of the facility by which people can honor him with their lips while their hearts are far removed from him (Mark 7:6). He warned in the Sermon on the Mount that on the last day people will say, "Lord, Lord" whom he will dismiss from his presence with the dreadful words, "I never knew you; depart from Me" (Matt. 7:23). In like manner James expounded the problem of those who declare they have faith but whose faith is moribund, yielding no fruit and displaying no works consistent with genuine saving faith (James 2:20).

Augustine's concept of the invisible church was not an ancient paradigm for an underground church or for a few loose groups

Fig. 1.1

The Visible and Invisible Church

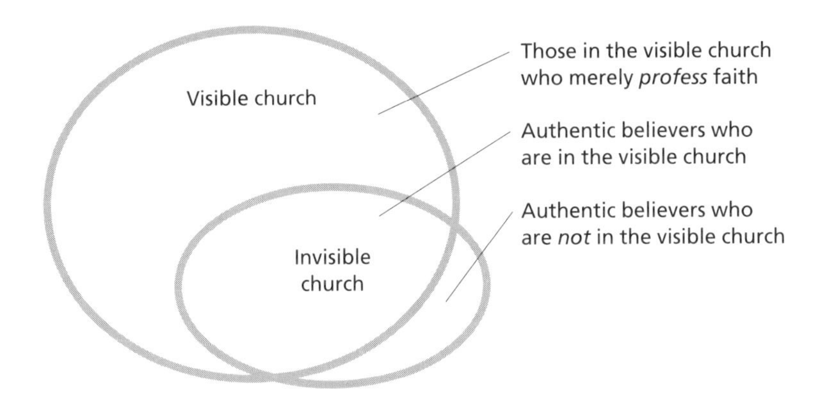

of people who do not join or participate in the life of an organized church or community of believers. For Augustine the term *invisible church* refers substantially to people who are inside the visible church. It refers to those within the visible church who are the wheat rather than the tares. It incorporates all who are in Christ Jesus. There are not two separate bodies, one inside the visible institution we call the organized church, and the other outside the parameters of the institutional church. Again, the invisible church is to be found *within* the visible church. We note, however, that Augustine spoke of the invisible church's being found *substantially* within the visible church. This differs from saying that the invisible church is contained exclusively within the visible church. Augustine recognized that for various reasons at various times, some members of the invisible church may not be within the visible church.

How is it possible for a person to be in the invisible church but not at the same time in the visible church? In the first instance we can point to individuals who have the desire to unite with a visible church but who are providentially hindered from doing so. Suppose, for example, a person is converted to Christ. On the way to join a local church, he is hit by a car or suffers a fatal heart attack and dies before he has the opportunity to do so. We think immediately of the thief on the cross who embraced Christ in his dying moments (assuming he was not a believer before that time) and received the comforting assurance from Jesus that he would soon join Jesus in paradise (Luke 23:43).

A second category includes people who in their spiritual infancy mistakenly believe it is not their duty to unite with a visible church. They may remain in error for a season, even though they are truly converted.

A third category includes those for whom there is no available visible church to join. This may involve prisoners in solitary confinement, those held in concentration camps, or people who live in isolated wilderness spots remote from any body of believers.

A fourth category includes believers who have been excommunicated from the visible church. It might surprise some that this category is even included. But it must be for the following reasons. First, the person may be the victim of an unjust excommunication. That is, the church may have erred in her judgment of excommunication and cast out a member who is wheat, mistaking him for a tare. Second, the person may have justly and properly been excommunicated while in a protracted period of impenitence, even though he is truly converted. Excommunication, among other things, is a final step of discipline for church members, but it carries the hope that it will lead the person to repentance, with him being restored to full fellowship. The classic case is the incestuous man of the Corinthian church (1 Cor. 5:1). While in the state of excommunication, the person is to be *regarded* as an unbeliever, yet with the understanding that the church can only look at the outward appearance while God alone can read his heart.

A fifth category includes those who are in the invisible church but are united with false or apostate visible institutions that claim to be churches. This category has posed a serious problem for the church of all ages. In antiquity heretical movements arose such as Montanism, Arianism, and Monophysitism, the leaders of which were declared heretics and banished from the visible church. Not all of these heretics went away quietly. Often they continued their false teaching and organized followers into "churches." Some of these heretical bodies captured true believers in their fold, at least for a season. This category recognizes that a member of the invisible church may for one reason or another be enrolled in a false visible church, which in reality is not a church.

Probably at no time in church history was the question more acute than during the catastrophic upheaval of the sixteenth-century Protestant Reformation. This resulted in the most severe fragmentation of the visible church in the history of Christendom. When Martin Luther was excommunicated by the Roman Catholic Church, was he therefore outside the invisible church? When Protestants organized into various groups such as Baptists, Lutherans, Reformed, and Episcopalians, were these groups valid churches or false churches? And what of Rome? Many of those who left the Roman Catholic Church in the sixteenth century did not hesitate to declare Rome apostate and therefore no longer a true church.

The issue became for Protestants not so much the question, What is *the* true church? Instead it was, What is *a* true church? Rome continued to assert that she was not only *a* true church, but *the* true church. That assertion was strongly challenged by Protestants. Again the challenge was not simply that Rome was not the true church, but that she was no longer a genuine visible church at all.

When Is a Church Not a Church?

In the ensuing years following the outbreak of the Reformation, various communions and sects arose that went in widely different directions. The question of what is a sect, a cult, or a bona fide church became critical to many people who earnestly desired to be faithful to Christ but found it difficult to discern the marks of a true visible church. Out of this conflict and the reflection it provoked came the historic Protestant view of the marks of a true church: (1) the preaching of the gospel, (2) the due administration of the sacraments, and (3) the presence of church discipline (which included some form of ecclesiastical government necessary to that end).

Fig. 1.2

The first mark was conceived in terms of not only the *practice* of preaching, but its *content*. In this regard the criterion was intensely theological. The concept of the "gospel" included the content of truth that is essential to biblical Christianity. For example, the content included the major tenets of historic Christian orthodoxy such as the Trinity, the deity of Christ, the atonement, and the resurrection. These affirmations were embodied in the classical creeds and confessions of the ancient ecumenical councils such as Nicea and Chalcedon. If an organization that rejected essential elements of historic, catholic Christianity claimed to be a church, this claim was rejected. In modern terms we ask the question, Is the Church of the Latter Day Saints a true church? Is the organization called Jehovah's Witnesses a true church? Certainly Mormons claim to be a church. Not only that, but they claim to be a *Christian* church. Jesus has a prominent role in their religion. He is venerated and elevated to a position of honor. Mormons even speak of having a "personal relationship" with Christ. Yet both Mormons and Jehovah's Witnesses categorically deny Christ's deity. Likewise the Trinity is denied by some groups organized as churches, such as the Unitarians.

Those who adhere to the marks of the church as formulated by the Protestant Reformers do not accept the bodies mentioned above because, not only are they infected by theological error or heresy, but their errors and heresies involve the rejection of truths or doctrines essential to biblical Christianity. These institutions, though claiming to be churches, are regarded as false churches, sects, or cults by orthodox Christianity.

Is it then possible for a true Christian to be a member of any of these institutions? The answer must be yes. Not every member of an institution affirms everything the institution formally affirms, or denies everything the institution denies. It is possible for a person to be a member of a Mormon community and still believe in the deity of Christ, just as it is possible for a person to be a member of a visible church that affirms the deity of Christ while privately rejecting this doctrine.

As late as the nineteenth century at Vatican Council I (1870), Rome referred to Protestants as schismatics and heretics. The tone of Rome changed dramatically in our own day at Vatican II (1965), where Protestants were referred to as "separated brethren." This was not a tacit recognition that Protestant churches are valid, but a clear affirmation that true believers can be found in institutions that have separated from Holy Mother Church.

When the Reformers declared Rome apostate and no longer a true church, they did so not because Rome denied the Trinity, the deity of Christ, his atonement, and his resurrection, all of which were deemed of the *esse* or essence of Christian truth, but because Rome condemned the doctrine of justification by faith alone or *sola fide.* The Reformers believed that *sola fide* is an essential truth of biblical Christianity. To deny this or any other essential truth would disqualify an institution from being a valid or true church. It was not as if the Reformers thought Rome was so apostate that she denied *all* the essential truths of biblical Christianity. On the contrary, they recognized that Rome retained and maintained her confession of many essential truths of Christianity.

For Luther the conviction that *sola fide* is "the article upon which the church stands or falls" was not an idle bit of bombast or a theological tilting at windmills. For him this was no tempest in a teapot or exercise in shadow-boxing. Nor could he be convinced that the whole controversy was simply a matter of an unfortunate or tragic misunderstanding among the parties involved. If ever a theological controversy received close and detailed scrutiny about what was being confessed and denied by the disputing parties, it was the controversy over justification.

If the church's condemnation of Arius was not based on a misunderstanding, it is even more certain that Rome's condemnation of *sola fide* was not based on a misunderstanding. To be sure, during the course of the controversy, as in the case of most such controversies, misunderstandings did occur, and at times they seemed to abound. Even a cursory reading of the canons of the sixth session of the Council of Trent reveals that, though there were still issues clouded by misunderstanding, the essential point of disagreement was not missed by either party.[1]

For Martin Luther and later John Calvin, the normative status of *sola fide* is crucial to the question of a true church versus an apostate church. They reasoned that *sola fide* is *essential* to the biblical gospel. When an essential truth of the gospel is condemned, the gospel itself is condemned with it, and without the gospel an institution is not a Christian church. This is simply another way of saying that the gospel is an essential, if not *the* essential, of biblical Christianity, and that it is the first mark of the church.

Rome was convinced that the gospel Luther and Calvin taught was a false gospel. That is precisely why Rome condemned *sola fide*. If she were correct, then her claim to be a true church and also *the* true church is vindicated, and it would be Luther, Calvin, and Protestants who were involved in apostate bodies. On the other hand, if Rome was wrong in condemning *sola fide*, she was condemning herself to apostasy.

If Rome is not a valid visible church, is it possible that within her membership there are Christians, members of the invisible church? Surely the answer to this question must be "Yes!" It is not only possible, but highly likely, especially in light of the cross-communication between Protestants and Catholics in our day, that there are multitudes of people within the Roman Catholic communion who belong to Christ and are a part of his mystical body, the church, if only in its invisible corporation.

When Must a Believer Dis-Unite?

A question that vexes many earnest Christians is this: When must they leave the fellowship of a visible church? The question is exacerbated in our times by the casual and cavalier manner in which Christians engage in "church-hopping," moving from one denomination to another. It is exacerbated in the other direction by the premium placed on church unity, guarding it at all cost regardless the loss of purity and truth. Some churches require their pastors to take a sacred vow to work for the peace, purity, and unity of the church. But if the church becomes impure in its doctrine or its practice and the pastor earnestly seeks to purify the church, he is almost always accused of disturbing the church's peace and unity. Such was the fate of the Old Testament prophets and the New Testament apostles, who discovered that to preserve all three equally, peace, purity, and unity, is a "mission impossible."

In reality churches often lapse into states of corruption and grievous error. To abandon a church because of minor impurities is to lack charity. No church is perfect in its purity, in either doctrine or practice. Patience and charity are called for when the church falters. Yet there is a point at which the believer not only may but must leave the communion of a visible church. That is when the church becomes so corrupt that it enters a state of apostasy. Apostasy occurs when a church denies an essential truth of the Christian faith. If, for example, the church denies the gospel or abandons the sacraments, it ceases to be a true church and the believer is obligated to withdraw from it.

There are circumstances when believers acknowledge that their communions have become apostate but insist on remaining within them in order to work for their restoration or reformation. These sentiments are indeed noble but often leave the believers in a state of chronic conflict.

Inseparably related to the unity that believers enjoy by virtue of their inclusion in the invisible church is the unity that serves as the very basis for inclusion in that church, namely, our union with Christ. With respect to our personal relationship with Christ, the New Testament makes use of two vital prepositions: *in (en)* and *into (eis)*. In the biblical call to faith we are summoned to believe "into Christ." When we exercise such faith, we become "in Christ" and Christ is in us. Though being in Christ is intensely personal and individual, it is never individualistic. Every individual who is personally united to Christ is at the same time personally united with every other person who is in Christ. This comprises the fullness of our mystical union with Christ and defines the reality of the communion of saints. The individual believer never lives in isolation but is always incorporated. A true Christian may be described as a Christian, Incorporated. We are incorporated because we are immediately placed within a corporate organism, the *vere corpus,* or the true body of Christ. The church then is not merely an organization; it is a living organism, made up of its various vital parts.

When the New Testament uses the metaphor of the body to describe the church, it speaks of a unity in diversity. The human body is composed of various parts that individually and together are functionally necessary to the health of the whole. The eye is as vital as the ear, though performing different functions. In the church there are different tasks and different gifts, all of which are vital to the church's well-being and are necessary for fulfilling its mission.

Beyond the diversity of gifts and functions in the church, there are other points of diversity. The church is made up of people, and people are different in a multitude of ways. People from all sorts of backgrounds, ethnic and socioeconomic, are bonded together in the church. All the diversity of human personality is represented. The church has people who are extroverted and introverted. Some are loquacious, while others are taciturn. In addition the church is composed of people who are at vastly different points in their spiritual pilgrimages and at widely diverse levels of personal sanctification.

There is a common goal of conformity—to the image of Christ. We are all called to imitate him, seeking his mind and obeying his rule. In this sense there is a call to uniformity. But this is not a drab, colorless uniformity that forces people into molds that rob them of their individuality. That sort of uniformity is not redemptive but dehumanizing. The goal of Christian sanctification is not the loss of personality or individuality such as promised in religions that seek the absorption of the self into some world-soul, by which the self is engulfed by the whole and swallowed up in oblivion. For the Christian this union with and conformity to Christ enhances his personal self, not annihilates it. The church is the ultimate embodiment of the motto *e pluribus unum.*

Christ's Prayer for Unity

In any discussion of Christian unity or of ecumenical aspirations, Christ's high-priestly prayer for unity in John 17 comes to the forefront. Our Lord prayed that his people might be one in a way that parallels the Son's unity with the Father (17:20–23). Obviously this does not entail a prayer for substantial ontological unity such as that enjoyed by the Godhead. But it surely encompasses an analogical unity of purpose and mission among Christ's disciples such as is found in the union of purpose and mission displayed between the Father and the Son, as well as the Holy Spirit. The trinitarian God never works at cross purposes (no pun intended) with himself.

Never is there a hint of conflict or fragmentation within the Godhead. The unity that exists there is eternally perfect and incapable of either augmentation or diminution. But such conflict and fragmentation does exist among us. Does this mean that the intercessory prayer of Christ has failed or been rendered ineffectual? Surely we can never assume that our Priest has failed us or that his intercessory work has been impotent. Christ's prayer for unity has an "already" and a "not yet" dimension to it. True unity already exists in the invisible church and is enjoyed in the here and now of Christian experience. There remains an eschatological hope whose fulfillment is certain for the saints in heaven, but unity among believers already exists in our mystical union with Christ.

This union indicates that we share one Lord. The New Testament, however, speaks of a threefold unity we are to seek, including "one Lord, one faith, one baptism" (Eph. 4:5). Of these three the second seems to be the greatest obstacle to ecumenical unity among adherents of various Christian communities.

What is the meaning of "one faith"? The term *faith* in the New Testament is multifaceted. Faith may refer to the individual's act

Fig. 1.3

The Unity of Believers

of believing, or it may refer to that which is believed, the content of that faith.

In contemporary terms Christians are believers. They believe essentially in the same God and in the same Christ, but they often differ widely regarding the full content of their doctrinal affirmations. In Christian nomenclature the term *faith* refers specifically to the doctrines or creeds espoused by believers. We sometimes speak of the "Christian faith"—indicating the sum and substance of our creedal affirmations. It is not by accident, for example, that the Apostles' Creed begins with the word *credo,* "I believe . . ."

In the second Evangelicals and Catholics Together initiative, *The Gift of Salvation,* one point of agreement reached by the participating Roman Catholics and Evangelicals is that saving faith involves more than mere intellectual assent.[2] Surely this reference to intellectual assent has in mind the Reformers' exposition of the nature of saving faith, that this faith has at least three essential elements, *notitia, assensus,* and *fiducia.* The second of these, *assensus,* refers to the believer's intellectual assent to something. But mere intellectual assent to certain truths is not enough. A bare intellectual assent to doctrine falls short of *fiducia,* a personal trust, which is necessary for justification.

Though the signatories of GOS agreed that saving faith involves *more* than mere intellectual assent, we must assume that they also tacitly agreed that saving faith does not involve *less* than *assensus.*

We have given a more full exposition of the elements of saving faith in *Faith Alone.*[3] For now let me repeat that these elements include aspects that are *necessary conditions* for justification, which in isolation from *fiducia* do not meet the level of *sufficient condition*. That is, though *notitia* and *assensus* are *necessary* for salvation, they are not enough to gain salvation.

To get to the problem of unity we must look not only at the questions of assent and trust *(assensus* and *fiducia)*, but also to the first element, *notitia*.

Notitia or, as it is sometimes described, *notae* refers to the content of faith, the data understood and affirmed by the mind. This simply means that saving faith has content. In believing, there must be something that we believe. Faith does not exist in a vacuum, or perhaps more accurately as a vacuum. A vacuous faith is an oxymoron.

The *notitia* contains the essential truths of the Christian faith, such as the existence, nature, and character of God, the person and work of Christ, and the nature of the gospel.

With respect to the latter, before we can believe the gospel we must have some idea of its content. Before we can have unity in the gospel, we must agree to what the gospel is.

The same may be true about God and Christ. For example, if a person "believes" in Christ in the sense that he affirms that Christ was merely a great human teacher of ethics who died as a moral example of the virtuous man, whose virtue is to be imitated by his followers but who offered no atonement, and who stayed dead without resurrection and ascension, is this "faith" in Jesus saving faith? Here the *notitia* of such faith falls short of biblical faith and leaves us with a gospel that is not the biblical gospel.

How one understands the person and work of Christ is critical to unity of faith and unity in the gospel. If we differ among ourselves at essential points regarding these matters, we have not achieved the unity of faith of which the Scriptures speak.

As we have seen, Evangelicals and Mormons do not share a unity of faith because they differ radically concerning the person of Christ. Such a problem does not exist (in the essentials) between Rome and Evangelicalism.

2

Evangelicals and the Evangel

British analytical philosopher Anthony Flew once told a parable to illustrate the crisis philosophers and theologians face in speaking meaningfully about God. So many diverse distinctions have been used in "God-talk" that Flew concluded the word *god* has suffered the "death of a thousand qualifications." This crisis in our language about God was in large part responsible for the so-called "Death of God" controversy of the 1960s.

Today we face a similar linguistic crisis with respect to the term *evangelical*. Has it also suffered the death of a thousand qualifications, to the point that it is no longer a descriptive category?

In a rudimentary way the term *evangelical* serves as a theological or ecclesiastical label. Labels are a kind of shorthand for placing people in certain ideological groups. We use terms like *liberal, conservative, classical,* and *orthodox* in such a manner. Or we refer more specifically to certain schools of thought, such as Calvinists, Arminians, Barthians, and dispensationalists.

With the facile use of such labels, we seek to categorize generic groups. Such labels can easily be abused because they speak in such broad terms.

On the other hand, in a certain sense *all* words are "labels." They are names we employ to identify objects, actions, and so forth. Words themselves are strange but powerful tools that make knowledge and communication possible. When we consider the dynamics of spoken and written words (or those indicated by sign language), we understand that in one sense all language is *sign language.* Words do not embody the thing described; they signify something beyond themselves. They point to objects, actions, or ideas.

When employing letters to make words, we arrange shapes in an orderly manner. Different languages are different forms or letters to create written words. For example, the English language uses a twenty-six–letter alphabet. The term *alphabet* itself is derived from the names of the first two letters of the Greek alphabet, *alpha* and *beta.*

The twenty-six letters of our alphabet we can arrange and rearrange to create hundreds of thousands of distinct words. Other language groups employ the same alphabet to form words. When considering the manifold languages that employ this alphabet, we can construct literally millions of words using the same twenty-six letters.

The individual letters of our alphabet are composed of written shapes. We form the letter A by using two vertical lines and one horizontal line. We add and combine curved lines to vertical and horizontal lines to form other letters. We can make a B with a vertical line and two curved lines. If we break down the formation of our twenty-six letters, we see that they are formed by only a handful of different shapes or forms, combined in various ways. Thus, if we can draw a few straight lines and a few curves, we can learn to print all of the words found in the English language.

Similarly there are only a few distinct sounds made by the human voice, sounds that can be arranged in a massive variety of ways to form the sounds of spoken language.

My wife and I took ballroom dancing lessons for five years. In our first lesson our instructor informed us that if we could walk we could dance. We soon discovered that the numerous complex patterns employed in sophisticated dances such as the tango, waltz, or cha-cha could be reduced to a handful of simple walking patterns combined in a wide variety of ways.

Words are the key to knowledge. They are a form of the science of taxonomy or classification. We learned the idea of taxonomy in high school biology when we were taught the differences between kingdom, phylum, class, order, genus, and species. The simple process of such classification, which is the root of all knowledge, is the process of noting *similarities* and *differences.* In biology we distinguish between the animal kingdom and the plant kingdom. We notice that though there is a difference between animals and plants, they share a common denominator: Both are made up of living things. The chief category of biology is the category of life. The term *biology* means literally "the word about" or "concept" or "logic" (*logos*) of life (*bios*).

Yet biology itself is a specific science that can be differentiated from other sciences such as physics, astronomy, or chemistry. Within the realm of biology, we can further differentiate between zoology (the study of animal life) and botany (the study of plant life).

All divisions of science are distinguished by taxonomy, which involves the consideration of both similarities and differences. For example, all mammals are animals, but not all animals are mammals.

What is true in biology is true for all language and knowledge. For a word to mean something, it must signify something that is individuated from something else. If all words signified the same thing, then our language and knowledge could be reduced to a single word. If words are to be meaningful, they must signify something that is different from something else. It is "this" and not "that."

I labor the elemental nature of language and word usage to illustrate the linguistic significance of a word like *evangelical.* If the term is to be meaningful, it must signify something specific that differs from other things. In popular usage *evangelical* signifies a species of the genus *Christian.* Therefore we often hear the term *evangelical Christian,* in which *evangelical* designates a particular kind of Christian.

To leap ahead for a moment, we must note in passing that the term *evangelical Christian* may be a redundancy. If in its rudimentary form the term *evangelical* means "gospel-believing," then it would seem redundant to speak of gospel-believing Christians. This would indicate that there are non–gospel-believing Christians, or Christians who do not believe the gospel, which *prima facie* sounds like a contradiction in terms. It is somewhat like the term *born-again Christian.* If all who are Christians are born again and all who are born again are Christians, the term *born-again Christian* would be redundant, involving the use of a distinction without a difference.

In the religious nomenclature of historic Christianity, however, there have been many who claim the term *Christian* who reject personal rebirth, or who reject the content of the evangel or gospel. It has been necessary for people to adopt such language to distinguish themselves theologically from those who claim the term *Christian* for themselves while denying these disputed elements of Christianity.

This is why it is naive in the extreme for people to declare, "I am simply a Christian; I won't use any other labels." This ignores two thousand years of the church's struggle to distinguish heresy from orthodoxy, true Christianity from false forms of or claims to Christian faith.

When lexicographers write dictionaries, their definitions involve three distinct aspects. The first is etymology, or the word's linguistic derivative. Let us use the term *antinomy* as an example. This word is formed by a prefix and a root derived from the Greek language. The prefix *anti* means "against" and the root *nomos* means "law." An *antinomy* then is something that is against some law. The law in view here is the law of contradiction. Originally the term *antinomy* referred to a statement or proposition that violates the law of contradiction and was therefore a synonym for *contradiction.* The English word *contradiction* is derived from the Latin prefix *contra* ("against") and the verb *dicio* ("to speak").

The term *evangelical* derives from the English *evangel,* which is in turn a transliteration of the Greek *evangelium,* which means "gospel." Thus the term *evangelical* etymologically refers to that which is of or pertains to the evangel, or gospel.

The second aspect of word definition is its historic usage or its classical meaning. In the case of *antinomy,* its historic or classical use has been chiefly in technical philosophical language. The word *antinomy* has been used (as in the case of Immanuel Kant) to refer to mutually exclusive or irreconcilable concepts. In other words, historically the term has functioned in a manner consistent with its derivation, as a synonym for *contradiction.*

The third aspect of word definition is contemporary or customary usage. We may conclude that is the most important consideration given by lexicographers for word definition. There is a simple but important reason for this. Language is dynamic, not static. People use the same words in different ways at different times. Language is always in a state of flux as subtle changes are gradually introduced by shifts of usage, often engendered by confusion or an imprecise use of words. If a word is misused long enough and widely enough, its misuse emerges as the new proper use.

Consider the word *scan,* for example. If I tell my students to scan the textbook, they usually take that to mean "skim lightly over the surface." Originally the term *scan* meant to look closely at things, a meaning retained by airport traffic controllers who employ a radar scan (we hope they do not skim lightly over the scene of the airport). The words *scan* and *skim* sound so similar and have been so confused in popular usage that what were once antonyms have become synonyms.

Likewise the term *antinomy* is now defined by some dictionaries as a synonym for *paradox.* Originally *paradox* referred to something that seemed or appeared to be a contradiction, but under closer scrutiny was seen not to be an actual contradiction. The etymology of *paradox* comes from the Greek *para* ("alongside of") and *dokein* ("to seem, appear," or "to think"). A paradox meant that, when placed alongside a contradiction, what seemed or appeared to be a contradiction actually was not. Historically and classically a *paradox* was something that differed from and could be distinguished from an antinomy or contradiction. Now the term *antinomy* is frequently listed as a synonym for *paradox*. This reflects what happens when word changes occur because of imprecise usage.

This shift in meaning and confusion of usage has occurred with a vengeance in the case of the term *evangelical*. The historic or classical use of the term has its roots in the Reformation controversy of the sixteenth century. The Reformers used the term *evangelical* to define their movement as it related to the central theological issue of the day, the doctrine of justification by faith alone. The magisterial Reformers insisted that the doctrine of *sola fide*, or justification by faith alone, is an issue that focuses on the gospel itself. Borrowing from the Apostle Paul's teaching in Galatians that there is only one gospel (Gal. 1:6–9), the Reformers believed that *sola fide* is essential to the gospel, that without *sola fide* one does not have the gospel.

The Reformers believed that in the controversy over *sola fide* nothing less than the gospel was at stake. John Calvin believed, for example, that in rejecting and condemning *sola fide* Rome was rejecting and condemning the gospel itself, so that in the Roman doctrine of justification the gospel was "ruined." As a result the Reformers called themselves *Evangelicals* to distinguish themselves from Roman Catholics. In this regard the term *Evangelical* functioned as a synonym for *Protestant*. To be a *Protestant* meant negatively to protest against the Roman view, and positively to adhere to the evangelical view of *sola fide*. Thus all Evangelicals were Protestants and all Protestants were Evangelicals.

In the course of history, the meaning of the term *evangelical* has undergone a significant evolution. It can no longer be assumed that in popular usage *evangelical* is a synonym for

Fig. 2.1

The Changing Meaning of the Word *Evangelical*

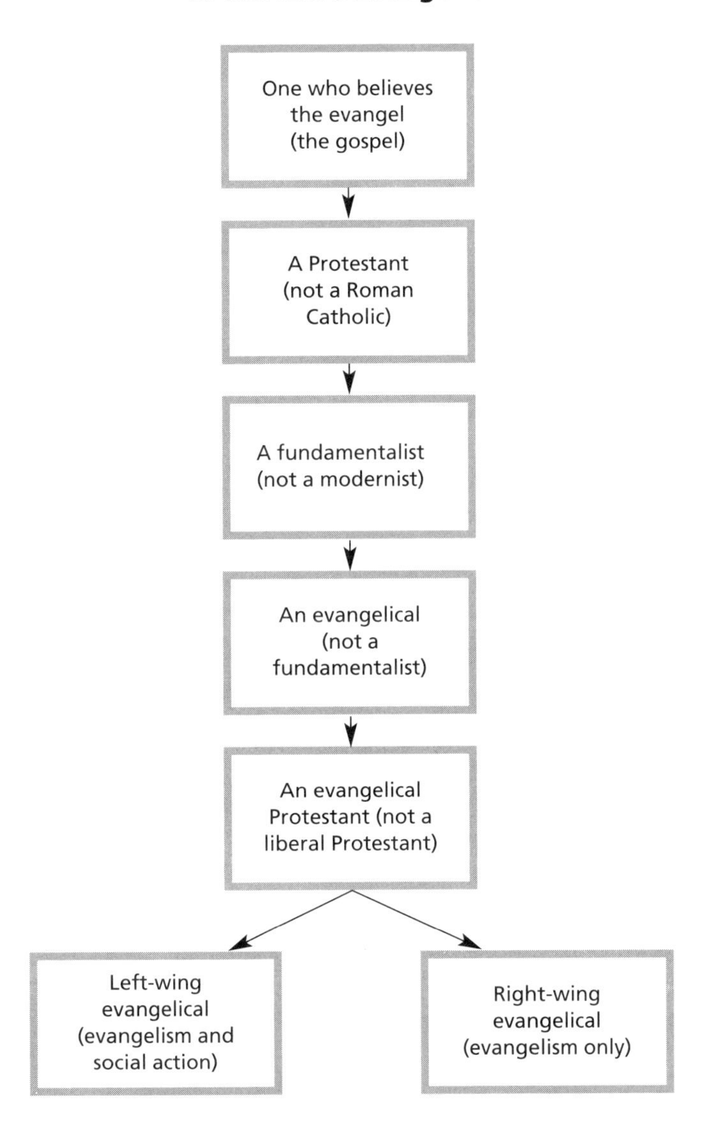

Protestant. In the twentieth century the chief distinction indicated by *evangelical* has been not so much to differentiate one's theological position from Rome's but rather to point to a specific position or group within Protestantism. That is, *evangelical* came to be used to describe a particular group *within* the Protestant community.

The Effect of Liberalism

This change in the popular usage of the term *evangelical* came about in large part due to the crisis precipitated in the ninteenth century by the advent of liberalism. The liberal movement in Protestantism rejected wholesale much of orthodox Christianity, particularly its supernatural elements. Questions were raised about New Testament miracles, about the virgin birth, atonement, resurrection, and deity of Christ. By the "gospel" liberals meant ethical values, and they saw the church's mission in terms of sociological and political "redemption." What emerged was the so-called Social Gospel, which advocated the humanitarian concern of working for a kingdom of God on earth that focuses on ethical values. The idea of personal reconciliation to God wrought by supernatural atonement and the regenerating inward work of God the Holy Spirit was eclipsed.

This led to the modernist-fundamentalist controversy that raged at the turn of the century. The fundamentalist movement was led chiefly by orthodox Christian scholars who sought to define the non-negotiable essence or fundamentals of historic Christianity. At the heart of fundamentalism was the desire to retain the biblical gospel and the mandate of Christ to his church to engage in the task of personal evangelism.

Parenthetically it is important to note that the label *fundamentalist* has also gone through significant changes. Where originally the driving force of fundamentalism was intellectual, orthodox scholars most of whom were Reformed in their theology, today *fundamentalism* usually carries the import of anti-intellectual moralism, which differs sharply from its historic meaning.

In the modernist controversy it was widely assumed that all Evangelicals were fundamentalists (because all Evangelicals embraced the fundamentals) and that all fundamentalists were Evangelicals, because *sola fide* was considered fundamental to biblical Christianity.

In a relatively short time many people began to call themselves Evangelicals rather than fundamentalists. There were various reasons for this. Not the least of these reasons was the desire to distance oneself from the pejorative connotations that had become attached to the word *fundamentalist.* The liberal critics did not tire of castigating fundamentalists as backwoods simpletons who lacked academic respectability and were theologically naive. Seminaries that held to such doctrines as the inerrancy of the Bible were particularly ridiculed. The psychological desire to escape such ridicule led many in the academic world to adopt the term *Evangelical* and to shun the term *fundamentalist.*

A second reason for the shift was that many conservatives who retained their belief in other fundamental doctrines abandoned their commitment to biblical inerrancy in light of the avalanche of biblical criticism. In this regard the shift in labels was due not to psychological preferences but to a real shift in theological conviction. A significant number of people who believed in *sola fide* and other elements of fundamentalism no longer were convinced that the Bible is inerrant.

This shift over the doctrine of Scripture was significant in light of historic Evangelicalism. Frequently historians single out two vital elements of the sixteenth-century Reformation as the causes of this movement. Following the ancient Aristotelian form-matter schema, historians refer to the Reformation's material cause as the debate over *sola fide* and its formal cause as the debate over *sola Scriptura.* In other words the Reformation debate focused not only on the issue of justification by faith alone, but also on the question of the basis for one's doctrine of justification as well as other doctrines.

In the course of his journey to the watershed Diet of Worms, Martin Luther engaged in two major disputations with Cardinal Cajetan and Johann Eck, in which Luther was shown to be in con-

Table 2.1

Causes of the Reformation

	Formal	Material
Latin name	*Sola Scriptura*	*Sola fide*
Translation	Scripture alone	Faith alone
Explanation	Scripture is the sole authority in doctrinal matters.	Justification is by grace alone through faith alone.

flict with both the teachings of the church councils and the authoritative teachings of the pope.

While Rome affirmed the inspiration and authority of the Bible, she also maintained a second source of special revelation: the tradition of the church. This dual source was confirmed at the Council of Trent, and this council also confirmed the authority of the church in biblical interpretation, disallowing any views that run counter to tradition. At Worms, when Luther was called on to recant his teaching, he replied that he could not unless convinced by sacred Scripture. Scripture alone, rather than tradition or church councils, has the authority to bind the conscience.

For centuries the twin affirmations of *sola Scriptura* and *sola fide* served as the glue unifying Evangelicals. These twin pillars made it possible for Evangelicals of different denominations to enjoy a high level of mutual cooperation and fellowship. Unified labor in evangelism and world missions has characterized historic Evangelicalism.

One of the sad results of the Reformation was the fragmentation of Protestantism into numerous denominations. Yet all of these diverse groups shared a common bond of doctrinal unity on two distinct levels. First, all Protestant creeds affirmed the common core of catholic Christianity as expressed in the ancient ecumenical councils, such as those of Nicea (325) and Chalcedon (451). Doctrines such as the Trinity and the dual nature of Christ were affirmed by all Protestant creeds. Second, all Protestant creeds also affirmed *sola Scriptura* and *sola fide*. What divided Protestants into various denominations were differences on the sacraments, church government, eschatology, and aspects of soteriology.

The rise of liberalism brought a creedal crisis over core catholic beliefs. Though few, if any, Protestant denominations altered their creeds to excise catholic doctrines such as the Trinity, many denominations stopped enforcing clerical subscription to the historic creeds, or refused to discipline clergy who denied these articles. One mainline denomination, when confronted with a clergyman who refused to affirm the deity of Christ and who denied the atonement, both (1) reaffirmed their historic creeds and (2) declared that the clergyman's views were within the limits of acceptable interpretation of these creeds. Now you see it; now you don't. The creeds were effectively relativized by adopting a view of "theological pluralism" that allows denial via "acceptable interpretation." Here we see a *de jure* orthodoxy coupled with a *de facto* apostasy.

This type of theological and confessional compromise reinforced the desire of some Protestants to differentiate themselves from members of their own communions by calling themselves Evangelicals. They remained evangelical in their doctrine.

In the twentieth century, due also in large measure to the impact of liberalism, another shift in the meaning of *evangelical* can be detected. To counteract the Social Gospel of modernism, people who believed in the need for personal salvation and in evangelism adopted the term *evangelical.* Confessional doctrines took a back seat to the task of evangelism. In some circles the task of evangelism became so emphasized that social concern was first neglected and then repudiated. To distance themselves from liberalism, many well-meaning Evangelicals began to suspect the legitimacy of the church's involvement in social issues. Since liberals reduced the church's mission to social concerns and eliminated personal evangelism, some were so zealous to promote evangelism that they began to view evangelism and social concern as an either/or dichotomy.

This dichotomy produced a rift within Evangelicalism between "left-wing" and "right-wing" Evangelicals. The "left-wing" insisted (correctly) that the relationship between personal evangelism and social concern is not either/or but both/and. The twentieth-century dichotomy between personal evangelism and social concern represented a somewhat bizarre departure from historic Christianity. For two millennia the church had understood her mission as involving both the proclamation of the gospel and the care of the poor, the widowed, the orphaned, the oppressed, and so forth. Only in reaction to liberalism did this anomaly emerge.

With the renewed emphasis on evangelism as defining Evangelicalism, the movement's doctrinal foundation began to erode. The cement that had bound Evangelicals together began to crack. This was seen in the first instance with the disintegration of *sola Scriptura* as a source of evangelical unity and solidarity. This left only one pillar standing, the doctrine of *sola fide.*

Recently we have witnessed the cracking of the pillar of *sola fide.* This has manifested itself in different ways. In the first place we saw a crisis break out in the dispensational wing of the evangelical community that spilled over into the broader evangelical community. This was the so-called Lordship-salvation controversy. This controversy revealed a sharp split in understanding of the doctrine of *sola fide.* Both sides in the dispute affirmed this doctrine, but they differed significantly in their understanding of it. This dispute revealed that there is no monolithic unity among professing Evangelicals in the matter of *sola fide.*

A less well-known dispute over a similar issue relating to *sola fide* emerged at Westminster Theological Seminary in Philadelphia when the faculty there differed over the orthodoxy of one professor regarding his doctrine of justification. This was significant because Westminster historically has been a bastion of Reformed orthodoxy and was one of the least likely places where one would expect such an issue to emerge. On the other hand it is precisely because Westminster has been so strong in its Reformed orthodoxy and has given so much care to Reformation doctrine that the slightest variance from orthodoxy would engender serious debate; at less zealous seminaries such issues would pass virtually unnoticed.

The Impact of ECT

The controversy surrounding the publication of *Evangelicals and Catholics Together*[1] heralded another subtle but significant shift in the contribution of *sola fide* to evangelical unity. When prominent members of the evangelical community publicly affirmed a unity of faith with their Roman Catholic cosigners, several questions emerged: (1) Had the Roman Catholic signatories rejected the Roman Catholic view of justification and embraced the Reformation view? (2) Had the Roman Catholic Church changed its doctrine of justification? (3) Had the evangelical signatories abandoned their view of *sola fide* and capitulated to the Roman Catholic view? (4) Had the Evangelicals who signed the document changed their view of *sola fide* to the extent that they no longer deemed it essential to the gospel and therefore to the Christian faith?

The answer to the first question is easy. The Roman Catholic signatories have made it clear that they have not abandoned their church's historic position. Keith Fournier, for example, has declared that he is an Evangelical, but in the orthodox Roman Catholic sense. That is, he defines the term *Evangelical* in its etymological sense, meaning one who believes the gospel. Of course historic Roman Catholicism has consistently maintained that it believes the gospel but that *sola fide* is not the gospel. Likewise, Richard John Neuhaus, the chief Roman Catholic architect of ECT, has made it clear that he still affirms the doctrines set forth at the Council of Trent.

Has the Roman Catholic Church changed her doctrines of justification and embraced the Reformation doctrine of *sola fide?* As I endeavored to show in my book *Faith Alone*,[2] I am convinced this is not the case. The new *Catechism of the Catholic Church*[3] reaffirms Trent in these issues. Certainly Rome has more toleration for *sola fide* today than she had in the sixteenth century, but her doctrine of justification has not changed in any significant manner.

Have the evangelical signatories of ECT abandoned their doctrine of justification and embraced the Roman Catholic view? I do not think so for a minute. Every evangelical signatory of ECT whom I know continues to affirm the doctrine of justification by faith alone.

The fourth question is the most crucial. Have the evangelical signatories of ECT abandoned the historic evangelical view, not of the doctrine of *sola fide,* but of its normativity and essentiality to the gospel? This was the question that sparked so much discussion and debate in the days following the ECT initiative. I am confident that now we can answer this question definitively. In light of the accord reached by the Committee for Evangelical Unity in the Gospel, which will be presented with commentary in part 3, it is clear that the answer to question four is "No!"

One benefit of controversy is that it forces people to sharpen their understanding of the issues in dispute. The controversy over ECT has had the salutary benefit of bringing the discussion of *sola fide* and the gospel onto center stage and putting it in bold relief. It is a marvelous thing to see and hear evangelical leaders discuss the meaning of *sola fide* and the gospel, and to witness a renewed passion for its truth and importance.

The labor of the past year by the Committee on Evangelical Unity in the Gospel, which grew out of the tensions following ECT, has witnessed a significant rally for the cause of the gospel among all the participants and a deepening of the historic bond we enjoy in the gospel. What began as a serious threat to evangelical unity has yielded a new appreciation for the essential bases of and for evangelical unity.

In the early days of discussion regarding ECT, the fear was voiced that the essential normative role of *sola fide* was being jeopardized. This was one motivating factor behind the second round of the ECT initiative, which culminated in the document *The Gift of Salvation*[4] (which we shall evaluate in part 2).

In the meantime the crisis moved such organizations as the Alliance of Confessing Evangelicals (ACE) to engage in efforts to salvage historic Evangelicalism. Its members describe themselves as "confessing Evangelicals" to indicate they use the term *evangelical* in its historic sense, as defined in the classic creeds and confessions of Reformation Christianity.

Table 2.2

Evangelical–Roman Catholic Statements

Title	Abbreviations	Date
Evangelicals and Catholics Together: The Christian Mission in the Third Millennium	ECT or ECT I	1994
The Gift of Salvation	GOS or ECT II	1997

If the qualifier *confessional* applied to Evangelicals is to have any meaning, it must signify something that sets it apart from non-confessional Evangelicals. What is a non-confessional Evangelical? It is someone who claims to be evangelical on some basis other than doctrine.

We hear of people who call themselves *evangelical* who at the same time say that doctrine does not matter. They are non-theological or even anti-theological Evangelicals. Since historic Evangelicalism was thoroughly doctrinal and confessional, this would signal a serious shift in the meaning of *evangelical*. In historic terms the idea of confessing Evangelicals would be a redundancy. But the term's historic meaning can no longer be assumed or taken for granted.

A person may consider himself an Evangelical if he employs evangelistic methods while eschewing the importance of evangelical doctrine. Or a person may call himself an Evangelical because he is associated with an evangelical tradition or institution. I heard a seminary professor talk about an evangelical scholar who rejects the sinlessness of Jesus. It begs the question how a person who holds such views, which depart from historic Evangelicalism, can be regarded as an "Evangelical."

If we define *evangelical* in accord with contemporary usage, then perhaps this term has suffered "the death of a thousand qualifications" and is no longer meaningful. I hope this is not the case and am confident the new document on evangelical unity, *The Gospel of Jesus Christ*,[5] will recapture the central affirmations of the gospel that are so vital to historic Evangelicalism.

Part 2

The Gift of Salvation: A Critical Analysis

The Gift of Salvation: Part 1

1. We confess together one God, the Father, the Son, and the Holy Spirit.
2. We can together bear witness to the gift of salvation in Jesus Christ.
3. The gravity of our plight and the greatness of God's love are brought home to us by the life, suffering, death, and resurrection of Jesus Christ.
4. God the Creator is also God the Redeemer, offering salvation to the world.
5. The present reality of salvation is an anticipation and foretaste of salvation in its promised fullness.
6. The work of redemption has been accomplished by Christ's atoning sacrifice on the cross.

3

Our Need for Justification

In October 1997 a group of Roman Catholic and evangelical leaders issued *The Gift of Salvation,*[1] a joint statement declaring their common understanding of the gospel and salvation. Since many of the framers of this document were also involved in the release of *Evangelicals and Catholics Together,*[2] this initiative has been popularly referred to as ECT II. This document "indicated an earnest attempt to state the message of salvation in such a way as to increase the hope of greater unity between Roman Catholics and Evangelicals." It was also a self-conscious attempt on the part of the original draftees of ECT to clarify their first document and to answer many of the objections that had been leveled against it.

ECT was considerably longer than ECT II and focused attention on a call to cobelligerency or cooperation between Evangelicals and Roman Catholics in the arena of what is often called "common grace." It called for a unified effort to stand against the tide of secularism and neopaganism that pervades our culture, particularly with regard to such issues as abortion, statism, human rights, and the relativization of truth.

In the context of this call for a united front in the sphere of cultural life, ECT affirmed a unity of faith and mission between Roman Catholics and Evangelicals, including an affirmation that we are justified by grace through faith because of Christ.

The document provoked much debate and discussion particularly because of the conspicuous absence of the word *alone*. Historic Evangelicalism has insisted that justification is by grace *alone (sola gratia)*, through faith *alone (sola fide)*, and because of Christ *alone (soli Christo)*.

Since the Roman Catholic Church has always affirmed that justification is by grace, through faith, and because of Christ but has firmly rejected the *solas* of the Reformation, many Evangelicals viewed this joint declaration as a sad and tragic compromise of the Reformation and of evangelical doctrine. Critical discussions of ECT focused on the absence of a clear affirmation of justification by faith alone *(sola fide)*, which has been the hallmark of historic Evangelicalism.

The Gift of Salvation (GOS) represents an effort to address this question. Many evangelical signatories were elated by the wording of GOS because they were convinced it achieved the goal of a joint declaration of *sola fide*.

This enthusiasm, however, was not shared by all Evangelicals. In early 1998 the Alliance of Confessing Evangelicals (ACE) released *An Open Letter of Pastoral Concern*,[3] which expressed the alliance's profound distress at both the assertions and omissions of GOS. Central to the assessment that GOS is seriously flawed is ACE's deep concern about the concept of imputation as it relates to justification by faith alone.

In addition to *An Open Letter*, ACE released its own summary statement regarding justification by faith alone.[4] Discussions between members of ACE and evangelical signatories of GOS have continued since that time, and the results have been encouraging.

Before offering a detailed analysis of GOS, we include the full text of this document.

††††††††††††

The Gift of Salvation

For God so loved the world that he gave his only Son, that whoever believes in him should not perish but have eternal life. For God sent the Son into the world, not to condemn the world, but that the world might be saved through him. (John 3:16–17)

We give thanks to God that in recent years many Evangelicals and Catholics, ourselves among them, have been able to express a common faith in Christ and so to acknowledge one another as brothers and sisters in Christ. We confess together one God, the Father, the Son and the Holy Spirit; we confess Jesus Christ the Incarnate Son of God; we affirm the binding authority of Holy Scripture, God's inspired Word; and we acknowledge the Apostles' and Nicene creeds as faithful witnesses to that Word.

The effectiveness of our witness for Christ depends upon the work of the Holy Spirit, who calls and empowers us to confess together the meaning of the salvation promised and accomplished in Christ Jesus our Lord. Through prayer and study of Holy Scripture, and aided by the Church's reflection on the sacred text from earliest times, we have found that, notwithstanding some persistent and serious differences, we can together bear witness to the gift of salvation in Jesus Christ. To this saving gift we now testify, speaking not for, but from and to, our several communities.

God created us to manifest his glory and to give us eternal life in fellowship with himself, but our disobedience intervened and brought us under condemnation. As members of the fallen human race, we come into the world estranged from God and in a state of rebellion. This original sin is compounded by our personal acts of sinfulness. The catastrophic consequences of sin are such that we are powerless to restore the ruptured bonds of union with God. Only in the light of what God has done to restore our fellowship with him do we see the full enormity of our loss. The gravity of our plight and the greatness of God's love are brought home to us by the life, suffering, death, and resurrection of Jesus Christ. "God so loved the world that he gave his only Son, that whoever believes in him should not perish but have eternal life" (John 3:16).

God the Creator is also God the Redeemer, offering salvation to the world. "God desires all to be saved and come to a knowledge of the truth" (1 Timothy 2:4). The restoration of communion with God is absolutely dependent upon Jesus Christ, true God and true man, for he is "the one mediator between God and men" (1 Timothy 2:5), and "there is no other name under heaven given among men by which we must be saved" (Acts 4:12). Jesus said, "No one comes to the Father but by me" (John 14:6). He is the holy and righteous one who was put to death for our sins, "the righteous for the unrighteous, that he might bring us to God" (1 Peter 3:18).

The New Testament speaks of salvation in various ways. Salvation is ultimate or eschatological rescue from sin and its consequences, the final state of safety and glory to which we are brought in both body and soul. "Since, therefore, we are now justified by his blood, much more shall we be saved by him from the wrath of God." "Salvation is nearer to us now than when we first believed" (Romans 5:9; 13:11). Salvation is also a present reality. We are told that "he saved us, not because of deeds done by us in righteousness, but in virtue of his own mercy" (Titus 3:5). The present reality of salvation is an anticipation and foretaste of salvation in its promised fullness.

Always it is clear that the work of redemption has been accomplished by Christ's atoning sacrifice on the cross. "Christ redeemed us from the curse of the law by becoming a curse for us" (Galatians 3:13). Scripture describes the consequences of Christ's redemptive work in several ways, among which are: justification, reconciliation, restoration of friendship with God, and rebirth from above by which we are adopted as children of God and made heirs of the Kingdom. "When the time had fully come, God sent his son, born of a woman, born under law, that we might receive the adoption of sons" (Galatians 4:4–5).

Justification is central to the scriptural account of salvation, and its meaning has been much debated between Protestants and Catholics. We agree that justification is not earned by any good works or merits of our own; it is entirely God's gift, conferred through the Father's sheer graciousness, out of the love that he bears us in his Son, who suffered on our behalf and rose from the dead for our justification. Jesus was "put to death for our trespasses and raised for our justification" (Romans 4:25). In justification, God, on the basis of Christ's righteousness alone, declares us to be no longer his rebellious enemies but his forgiven friends, and by virtue of his declaration it is so.

The New Testament makes it clear that the gift of justification is received through faith. "By grace you have been saved through faith; and this is not your own doing, it is the gift of God" (Ephesians 2:8). By faith, which is also the gift of God, we repent of our sins and freely adhere to the gospel, the good news of God's saving work for us in Christ. By our response of faith to Christ, we enter into the blessings promised by the gospel. Faith is not merely intellectual assent but an act of the whole person, involving the mind, the will, and the affections, issuing in a changed life. We understand that what we here affirm is in agreement with what the Reformation traditions have meant by justification by faith alone *(sola fide)*.

In justification we receive the gift of the Holy Spirit, through whom the love of God is poured forth into our hearts (Romans 5:5). The grace of Christ and the gift of the Spirit received through faith (Galatians 3:14) are experienced and expressed in diverse ways by different Christians and in different Christian traditions, but God's gift is never dependent upon our human experience or our ways of expressing that experience.

While faith is inherently personal, it is not a purely private possession but involves participation in the body of Christ. By baptism we are visibly incorporated into the community of faith and committed to a life of discipleship. "We were buried therefore with him by baptism into death, so that as Christ was raised from the dead by the glory of the Father, we too might walk in newness of life" (Romans 6:4).

By their faith and baptism, Christians are bound to live according to the law of love in obedience to Jesus Christ the Lord. Scripture calls this the life of holiness, or sanctification. "Since we have these promises, dear friends, let us purify ourselves from everything that contaminates body and spirit, perfecting holiness out of reverence for God" (2 Corinthians 7:1). Sanctification is not fully accomplished at the beginning of our life in Christ, but is progressively furthered as we struggle, with God's grace and help, against adversity and temptation. In this struggle we are assured that Christ's grace will be sufficient for us, enabling us to persevere to the end. When we fail, we can still turn to God in humble repentance and confidently ask for, and receive, his forgiveness.

We may therefore have assured hope for the eternal life promised to us in Christ. As we have shared in his sufferings, we will share in his final glory. "We shall be like him, for we shall see him as he is" (1 John 3:2). While we dare not presume upon the grace of God, the promise of God in Christ is utterly reliable, and faith in that promise overcomes anxiety about our eternal future. We are bound by faith itself to have firm hope, to encourage one another in that hope, and in such hope we rejoice. For believers "through faith are shielded by God's power until the coming of the salvation to be revealed in the last time" (1 Peter 1:5).

Thus it is that as justified sinners we have been saved, we are being saved, and we will be saved. All this is the gift of God. Faith issues in a confident hope for a new heaven and a new earth in which God's creating and redeeming purposes are gloriously fulfilled. "Therefore God has highly exalted him and bestowed on him the name which is above every name, that at the name of Jesus every knee should bow, in heaven and on earth and under the earth, and every tongue confess that Jesus Christ is Lord, to the glory of God the Father" (Philippians 2:9–11).

As believers we are sent into the world and commissioned to be bearers of the good news, to serve one another in love, to do good to all, and to evangelize everyone everywhere. It is our responsibility and firm resolve to bring to the whole world the tidings of God's love and of the salvation accomplished in our crucified, risen, and returning Lord. Many are in grave peril of being eternally lost because they do not know the way to salvation.

In obedience to the Great Commission of our Lord, we commit ourselves to evangelizing everyone. We must share the fullness of God's saving truth with all, including members of our several communities. Evangelicals must speak the gospel to Catholics and Catholics to Evangelicals, always speaking the truth in love, so that "working hard to maintain the unity of the Spirit in the bond of peace . . . the body of Christ may be built up until we all reach unity in the faith and in the knowledge of the Son of God" (Ephesians 4:3, 12–13).

Moreover, we defend religious freedom for all. Such freedom is grounded in the dignity of the human person created in the image of God and must be protected also in civil law.

We must not allow our witness as Christians to be compromised by half-hearted discipleship or needlessly divisive disputes. While we rejoice in the unity we have discovered and are confident of the fundamental truths about the gift of salvation we have affirmed, we recognize that there are necessarily interrelated questions that require further and urgent exploration. Among such questions are these: the meaning of baptismal regeneration, the Eucharist, and sacramental grace; the historic uses of the language of justification as it relates to imputed and transformative righteousness; the normative status of justification in relation to all Christian doctrine; the assertion that while justification is by faith alone, the faith that receives salvation is never alone; diverse understandings of merit, reward, purgatory, and indulgences; Marian devotion and the assistance of the saints in the life of salvation; and the possibility of salvation for those who have not been evangelized.

On these and other questions, we recognize that there are also some differences within both the Evangelical and Catholic communities. We are committed to examining these questions further in our continuing conversations. All who truly believe in Jesus Christ are brothers and sisters in the Lord and must not allow their differences, however important, to undermine this great truth, or to deflect them from bearing witness together to God's gift of salvation in Christ. "I appeal to you, brothers, in the name of our Lord Jesus Christ, that all of you agree with one another so that there may be no divisions among you and that you may be perfectly united in mind and thought" (1 Corinthians 1:10).

As Evangelicals who thank God for the heritage of the Reformation and affirm with conviction its classic confessions, as Catholics who are conscientiously faithful to the teaching of the Catholic Church, and as disciples together of the Lord Jesus Christ who recognize our debt to our Christian forebears and our obligations to our contemporaries and those who will come after us, we affirm our unity in the gospel that we have here professed. In our continuing discussions, we seek no unity other than unity in the truth. Only unity in the truth can be pleasing to the Lord and Savior whom we together serve, for he is "the way, the truth, and the life" (John 14:6).

† † † † † † † † † † † †

The Gift of Salvation requires careful scrutiny, paragraph by paragraph.

A Common Faith in Christ

"For God so loved the world that he gave his only Son, that whoever believes in him should not perish but have eternal life. For God sent the Son into the world, not to condemn the world, but that the world might be saved through him." (John 3:16–17)

[1] We give thanks to God that in recent years many Evangelicals and Catholics, ourselves among them, have been able to express a common faith in Christ and so to acknowledge one another as brothers and sisters in Christ. We confess together one God, the Father, the Son and the Holy Spirit; we confess Jesus Christ the Incarnate Son of God; we affirm the binding authority of Holy Scripture, God's inspired Word; and we acknowledge the Apostles' and Nicene creeds as faithful witnesses to that Word.

The Gift of Salvation begins with John 3:16–17 followed by an opening paragraph in which the authors thank God for their ability to express a common faith in Christ and to acknowledge each other as brothers and sisters in Christ.

This acknowledgment was heralded in ECT and seen by Richard John Neuhaus as a major breakthrough in evangelical and Roman Catholic relations. It represents a significant shift in the tone of language used historically by the two groups, as well as a significant adjustment in attitude. For example, Vatican I (1870) described Protestants as "schismatics and heretics." Vatican II (1965), however, referred to Protestants as "separated brethren." For the Roman Catholic signatories of ECT to embrace Evangelicals as brothers and sisters in Christ is consistent with Vatican II statements.

On the other hand, though historic Evangelicalism has virtually always agreed that there are true Christians within the Roman Catholic Church, the basic judgment of Evangelicals is that Rome, as an institution, is apostate. Intermarriage between Catholics and Evangelicals has been and remains in some evangelical churches prohibited on the grounds that it involves the marriage of a believer to an unbeliever. The issue has focused on the relationship of *sola fide* to the gospel and the necessity of believing the essence of the gospel in order to be a Christian.

Historically Evangelicals have not taught that justification is based on believing the right doctrine. The doctrine of *sola fide* does not save anyone. A person can affirm this doctrine without possessing true saving faith in Christ and the gospel. But the question remains, Can one believe the gospel while at the same time rejecting *sola fide?* If *sola fide* is essential to the gospel, then it would seem that to reject it would be to reject the gospel's essence. Can an Evangelical embrace people who reject *sola fide* and consider them to be brothers and sisters in Christ? Surely there are individuals within Rome who do not reject *sola fide* as their church does and who embrace the true gospel. Those individuals are surely part of the invisible church and are our brothers and sisters in Christ.

Since so much of the dispute about Christian fellowship of brothers and sisters in Christ focuses now, as it did in the sixteenth century, on the doctrine of *sola fide,* the affirmation of this doctrine in GOS is of paramount importance. Charles Colson has been quoted as saying that he would not sign GOS unless it clearly affirmed *sola fide.*[5] Evangelicals who have signed or embraced

GOS have, as far as I know, not abandoned their commitment to *sola fide,* and they are satisfied that in fact GOS affirms *sola fide.* Those of us who are less sanguine about GOS are not satisfied that it does. We will analyze the reasons for this dissatisfaction later, but for now we simply note it in passing.

Paragraph 1 goes on to affirm doctrines that have been mutually affirmed by Catholics and Evangelicals for centuries such as the Trinity, the Incarnation, the binding authority of Scripture as God's inspired Word, and it embraces the Apostles' and Nicene creeds.

Though Rome has historically maintained the binding authority of the inspired Scripture, she has rejected the evangelical doctrine of *sola Scriptura.* Nothing is said of this issue in paragraph 1. The historic differences over the content of the canon are also passed over without comment, leaving open the question of what constitutes Scripture. The Roman canon has 80 books, including the Apocrypha, while the evangelical canon has 66 books.

The Meaning of Salvation

> [2] The effectiveness of our witness for Christ depends upon the work of the Holy Spirit, who calls and empowers us to confess together the meaning of the salvation promised and accomplished in Christ Jesus our Lord. Through prayer and study of Holy Scripture, and aided by the Church's reflection on the sacred text from earliest times, we have found that, notwithstanding some persistent and serious differences, we can together bear witness to the gift of salvation in Jesus Christ. To this saving gift we now testify, speaking not for, but from and to, our several communities.

This paragraph affirms that our witness for Christ depends on the work of the Holy Spirit, which both groups have historically affirmed. A second clause is added that reads, "who calls and empowers us to confess together the meaning of . . . salvation." Does *us* refer to the framers and signatories of GOS? If so, the architects of this document are asserting that they produced it under the calling and empowering of the Holy Spirit. I take the document's words to say that it was written in answer to the Holy

Spirit's call and by his empowerment. If that is true, then to reject GOS would do violence to God's Spirit. If that is not true, then such a claim would likewise do violence to the Spirit.

The document goes on to say that the efforts of the writers included prayer, the study of Scripture, and the aid of "the Church's reflection on the sacred text from earliest times." Some Evangelicals have objected that "the Church's reflection" is a thinly veiled reference to the authority of tradition. I think this criticism is unfair. GOS makes no appeal to tradition's authority, only to its aid. Evangelicals also make use of the church's collective wisdom in seeking to understand Scripture, though without elevating this tradition to the level of binding authority. In paragraph 2 neither the evangelical nor the Roman Catholic participants were required to compromise their own historic positions.

Paragraph 2 ends with a statement that reiterates what was said in ECT, that the writers are speaking not for, but from and to, their several communities. This declaration emphasizes that GOS is not an official document of the Roman Catholic Church nor of any evangelical body. It represents the work of individuals who speak for themselves, *from* and *to* their respective communities.

These two prepositions, *from* and *to,* raise one important point of concern. Another preposition must be added to the equation: *about.* The document speaks *about* the writers' respective communions. This initiative certainly involves more than a joint declaration about what a handful of Roman Catholics and Evangelicals agree on. It functions more as a manifesto, which by its wide distribution seeks to declare far more broadly *about* Catholics and Evangelicals.

In a letter to *Christianity Today,* three signatories of GOS, Timothy George, Thomas C. Oden, and J. I. Packer, write: "We evangelicals who signed *The Gift of Salvation* do not claim a unity of faith with the church of Rome. What we do acknowledge is a unity in Christ with Roman Catholic believers who, no less than we ourselves, have been saved by God's grace and justified by faith alone. Despite our doctrinal differences, we who by faith know, love, trust, and hope in Christ the Mediator are brothers and sisters in the Lord."[6]

The Fallen Human Race

[3] God created us to manifest his glory and to give us eternal life in fellowship with himself, but our disobedience intervened and brought us under condemnation. As members of the fallen human race, we come into the world estranged from God and in a state of rebellion. This original sin is compounded by our personal acts of sinfulness. The catastrophic consequences of sin are such that we are powerless to restore the ruptured bonds of union with God. Only in the light of what God has done to restore our fellowship with him do we see the full enormity of our loss. The gravity of our plight and the greatness of God's love are brought home to us by the life, suffering, death, and resurrection of Jesus Christ. "God so loved the world that he gave his only Son, that whoever believes in him should not perish but have eternal life" (John 3:16).

This paragraph discusses the purpose of God in creating man and the ruination of the human race via man's fall. It stresses the gravity of our plight and the work of God to redeem us from our fallen state. These are points about which, as far as they go, have not been disputed historically by Evangelicals and Catholics, though the full extent of original sin has been.

Christ's Atoning Sacrifice

[4] God the Creator is also God the Redeemer, offering salvation to the world. "God desires all to be saved and come to a knowledge of the truth" (1 Timothy 2:4). The restoration of communion with God is absolutely dependent upon Jesus Christ, true God and true man, for he is "the one mediator between God and men" (1 Timothy 2:5), and "there is no other name under heaven given among men by which we must be saved" (Acts 4:12). Jesus said, "No one comes to the Father but by me" (John 14:6). He is the holy and righteous one who was put to death for our sins, "the righteous for the unrighteous, that he might bring us to God" (1 Peter 3:18).

[5] The New Testament speaks of salvation in various ways. Salvation is ultimate or eschatological rescue from sin and its consequences, the final state of safety and glory to which we are brought in both body and soul. "Since, therefore, we are now justified by his blood, much more shall we be saved by him from the wrath of God." "Salvation is

nearer to us now than when we first believed" (Romans 5:9; 13:11). Salvation is also a present reality. We are told that "he saved us, not because of deeds done by us in righteousness, but in virtue of his own mercy" (Titus 3:5). The present reality of salvation is an anticipation and foretaste of salvation in its promised fullness.

[6] Always it is clear that the work of redemption has been accomplished by Christ's atoning sacrifice on the cross. "Christ redeemed us from the curse of the law by becoming a curse for us" (Galatians 3:13). Scripture describes the consequences of Christ's redemptive work in several ways, among which are: justification, reconciliation, restoration of friendship with God, and rebirth from above by which we are adopted as children of God and made heirs of the Kingdom. "When the time had fully come, God sent his son, born of a woman, born under law, that we might receive the adoption of sons" (Galatians 4:4–5).

These three paragraphs are mostly biblical quotations concerning no particular matters of serious debate. They serve as preparation for the document's exposition of justification.

The Gift of Salvation: Part 2

7. Justification is entirely God's gift, conferred through the Father's sheer graciousness, out of the love that he bears us in his Son.
8. The gift of justification is received through faith.
9. In justification we receive the gift of the Holy Spirit, through whom the love of God is poured forth into our hearts.
10. Faith involves participation in the body of Christ.
11. Sanctification is progressively furthered as we struggle, with God's grace and help, against adversity and temptation.
12. We may have assured hope for the eternal life promised to us in Christ.

4

The Basis of Our Justification

Having established a foundation for a statement on justification, *The Gift of Salvation* plunges into this doctrine in the next paragraph.

Not Earned by Good Works

[7] Justification is central to the scriptural account of salvation, and its meaning has been much debated between Protestants and Catholics. We agree that justification is not earned by any good works or merits of our own; it is entirely God's gift, conferred through the Father's sheer graciousness, out of the love that he bears us in his Son, who suffered on our behalf and rose from the dead for our justification. Jesus was "put to death for our trespasses and raised for our justification" (Romans 4:25). In justification, God, on the basis of Christ's righteousness alone, declares us to be no longer his rebellious enemies but his forgiven friends, and by virtue of his declaration it is so.

In paragraph 7 we have statements that have been greeted by many Evangelicals with great enthusiasm. The paragraph declares: "We agree that justification is not earned by any good works or merits of our own; it is entirely God's gift. . . ."

Frequently well-meaning Evangelicals caricature Roman Catholic theology. They say Evangelicals believe that justification is by faith, Rome that justification is by works; Evangelicals believe that justification is by grace, and Rome that it is by merit. The issue of faith versus works and grace versus merit has been a perennial bone of contention.

In paragraph 7 it sounds like Roman Catholics are eschewing the role of works and merit in justification altogether. But this requires a closer look. What GOS says is that justification is not *earned* by good works or merits of our own. Is this statement one that an orthodox Roman Catholic can endorse? Or does it indicate a significant shift away from Roman orthodoxy?

Rome teaches that though good works are necessary for justification, these works, strictly speaking, do not *earn* justification. Rome teaches that for persons to be justified they must have true righteousness inhering in them. Without good works there is no inherent righteousness, and without inherent righteousness there is no justification. These necessary good works are truly good works, but they result from God's gracious infusion of Christ's righteousness into the believer, grace that is received sacramentally. Since these works flow out of God's prior grace by virtue of the believer's cooperation with and assent to it, they are not the result of man's unaided efforts. Because these works rest and depend on God's grace, they do not, strictly speaking, earn salvation or justification.

When Rome speaks of merit with respect to justification, she is careful to speak of "congruous merit." This relates to the sacrament of penance, which Rome describes as the second plank of justification for those who have made shipwreck of their souls by mortal sin. The grace of justification received at baptism is lost or "killed" by mortal sin (that is why it is called "mortal") and is revived via penance. The sacrament of penance requires the performance of *works of satisfaction,* works that are necessary for a person's restoration to a state of grace and to justification, and works that yield *congruous merit (meritum de congruo)*. Congruous merit is a lower level of merit. It does not impose on God an obligation to reward it, but merely makes it "fitting" or "congruous" for God to reward it. Again, strictly speaking, congruous merit, though real and necessary, does not "earn" justification.

We notice also that paragraph 7 does not explicitly deny that we have merit, as Martin Luther emphatically did in rejecting both condign and congruous merit. The paragraph is phrased in such a way that it may include the possibility that we possess merits of our own. The statement does not say that we have no merits of our own, only that justification is not earned by merits of our own.

A Gift from God

The statement goes on to affirm that justification is entirely God's gift, inferred by the phrase "sheer graciousness." Statements like this sound very evangelical, seeing justification as a gift and one conferred by sheer graciousness. This, however, is completely consistent with historical, orthodox Roman Catholic theology. As long as justification is not earned and is rooted in God's grace, it may be called a gift. If it is not merited absolutely, then its conferring rests on sheer grace alone. This is consistent with Rome's view of *sola gratia*.

The last sentence of paragraph 7 has also occasioned evangelical rejoicing. One evangelical signatory of GOS called this statement the greatest breakthrough in Roman Catholic–evangelical dialogue in the last one hundred years. He was excited because, as he related to me, in this sentence the document affirms the evangelical doctrine of *forensic justification* and affirms categorically that our justification is based on the righteousness of Christ *alone*. The statement reads: "In justification, God, on the basis of Christ's righteousness alone, declares us to be no longer his rebellious enemies but his forgiven friends, and by virtue of his declaration it is so."

At first glance this sentence may appear to affirm the evangelical doctrine of forensic justification. But does it really? I think not. When Evangelicals speak of forensic justification, they mean that our justification is effected when God declares us just by virtue of the legal imputation of Christ's righteousness to our account. Justification is "forensic" in that it is the result of a legal declaration by God. We are justified when God declares us just. And certainly by virtue of the divine declaration, it is so that we are justified.

It is crucial, however, that we not overlook the unassailable fact that Rome also has her version of "forensic justification." She has always maintained that we are justified when God declares us just. It has never been in doubt or in question that justification is a divine act and that it is God and not someone else who declares us just in his sight. God is the Justifier.

The raging issue of the Reformation was the *ground* by which God declares us just. The Reformers insisted that the sole ground of our justification is the righteousness of Christ wrought *for* us in his life of perfect obedience. This is done by *imputation*. This means that God transfers to our account the righteousness of Christ wrought in his own person and that this righteousness is "counted" or "reckoned" to us by imputation.

Rome, on the other hand, believes God will declare just only those who really are just, who are inherently just. What Rome rejects is Luther's *simul iustus et peccator*. In this formula Luther declared that believers are "at the same time just and sinner." We are just by virtue of the fact that Christ's righteousness has been imputed to us, an act that takes place the moment we put our faith in Christ, and thus *before* we have been sanctified to the point that we are no longer sinners.

Rome rejects this view of justification as involving a "legal fiction" in which God declares people to be just who are not really just. For Rome God only declares people to be just when in fact they are just. This is the issue that sharply divides the gospel of Rome from the evangelical gospel. At the heart of the "good news" of the gospel is that God justifies us while we are still sinners.

GOS, however, explicitly declares that we are justified "on the basis of Christ's righteousness alone." In this bold assertion the evangelical signatories hear a clear affirmation of *sola fide.* What else could this mean except the evangelical doctrine?

The answer is that it can also mean the Roman Catholic doctrine, depending on how one understands the words. What is conspicuous by its absence in this affirmation is the word *imputed.* If the document stated that justification is "on the basis of *the imputation of* Christ's righteousness alone," then we would have an evangelical affirmation.

Remember that the chief aspect of justification disputed during the Reformation was the *ground* of our justification. According to the Reformers it is the *imputed* righteousness of Christ; according to Rome it is the *infused* righteousness of Christ. Both sides claimed that justification is based on the righteousness of Christ. They differed sharply and persistently over the question of imputed versus infused righteousness.

What is the difference? For Rome the infused righteousness of Christ, the grace of justification, is "poured into the soul" sacramentally. A person can be neither just nor justified without this infusion. But still the person must cooperate and assent to this infused righteousness to such an extent that righteousness actually inheres in the person. Only when the person is inherently just by the help of the grace of Christ's infused righteousness will God declare the person just.

Hence the issue was this: Is our justification based on the righteousness of Christ *in* us or the righteousness of Christ *for* us? Luther insisted that the righteousness by which we are justified is a righteousness that is *extra nos,* "apart from us." He called it an *iustitium alienum,* an "alien righteousness."

The Reformation doctrine is one of *synthetic* justification, meaning simply that we are justified by virtue of something added to our person that is not inherently ours. In contrast, the Roman view is one of *analytical* justification, by which we are declared to be just because analysis indicates we truly are just.

The great controversy of the sixteenth century over imputed versus infused righteousness is side-stepped in GOS. An orthodox Roman Catholic could in good conscience subscribe to this statement as long as the nature of Christ's righteousness (imputed or infused) is left unspecified.

When some Evangelicals, such as members of the Alliance of Confessing Evangelicals, registered their concern that the evangelical doctrine of imputation was not affirmed in GOS, it was stated by at least one GOS signatory that the Evangelicals who opposed ECT had now "moved the goal posts." This revealed a frustration growing out of the complaint that ECT failed to affirm *sola fide,* and now that GOS does affirm *sola fide* its detractors have moved the goal posts to focus on the issue of *imputation.*

The goal posts, however, have not been moved. Without imputation you do not have *sola fide. Sola fide* is still the issue. Just as *sola fide* is essential to the gospel, so imputation is essential to *sola fide.* In summary we believe that imputation is essential to the gospel and that without it you do not have the gospel or gospel unity.

It is important to note that GOS neither affirms nor denies imputation. In fact, as we will see later, the matter of imputation is left on the table for future discussion. Our concern is this: Unless or until the issue of imputation versus infusion is resolved, it is premature to declare a unity of faith and mission between Roman Catholics and Evangelicals.

The Response of Faith

> [8] The New Testament makes it clear that the gift of justification is received through faith. "By grace you have been saved through faith; and this is not your own doing, it is the gift of God" (Ephesians 2:8). By faith, which is also the gift of God, we repent of our sins and freely adhere to the gospel, the good news of God's saving work for us in Christ. By our response of faith to Christ, we enter into the blessings promised by the gospel. Faith is not merely intellectual assent but an act of the whole person, involving the mind, the will, and the affections, issuing in a changed life. We understand that what we here affirm is in agreement with what the Reformation traditions have meant by justification by faith alone *(sola fide).*

It is paragraph 8 that has convinced many that GOS has achieved a major breakthrough for unity between Roman Catholics and Evangelicals. This paragraph is seen as a joint affirmation of justification by faith alone. This paragraph affirms the following points:

1. Justification is received through faith.
2. Faith is a gift of God.
3. By our response of faith, we enter into the blessings promised by the gospel.
4. Faith is not mere intellectual assent.
5. Faith is an act of the whole person, involving the mind, the will, and the affections.
6. Faith results in a changed life.
7. What is here affirmed is in agreement with what the Reformation traditions have meant by justification by faith alone *(sola fide)*.

Let us begin our analysis by looking first at point 7. This sentence is worded somewhat awkwardly if it is intended to affirm *sola fide* itself. If that were the intent, it would have been simpler and much clearer to say, "What we here affirm is the Reformation view of *sola fide.*" Instead the document says merely that the elements affirmed are "in agreement" with *sola fide.* It is no mere quibble to point out the radical difference between saying that certain things agree with *sola fide* and saying that they actually add up to *sola fide.* To be in agreement simply requires that some aspects contained in *sola fide* are agreeable to both parties, that there are certain common points of affirmation found in both the Roman Catholic doctrine of justification and the evangelical doctrine of *sola fide.*

To clarify this, let us look at an analogy. Consider the historical dispute between the orthodox view of the person of Christ and the Mormon view. Mormons deny the eternality and deity of Christ. For them Christ is the highest and most exalted creature. He was the first creature created by God, and he pre-existed the world.

On the other hand, orthodox Christianity affirms that Christ is coeternal and cosubstantial with the Father. He is not a creature but fully God. Orthodoxy affirms the pre-existence of Christ precisely because he is eternal and the world is not.

The two views of Christ are mutually exclusive and include irreconcilable differences. Yet there is at least one point on which both parties agree: the pre-existence of Christ. Does this point of agreement indicate that the two parties share a common faith in Christ? By no means. Orthodoxy sees the deity of Christ as essential to a sound Christology, so that without it you do not have the orthodox view of Christ.

Likewise if the Roman Catholic view of justification has points of agreement with the evangelical view but differs at essential points, then Roman Catholics and Evangelicals do not share a common doctrine of justification.

Faith Alone?

Let us look more closely at the specific points that GOS affirms and that it says are in agreement with *sola fide.*

1. Justification is received through faith. The Roman Catholic Church has always affirmed that justification is by faith in the sense that faith is a necessary condition (though not a sufficient condition) for justification. The Council of Trent declared that faith is the beginning *(initium),* the foundation *(fundamentum),* and the root *(radix)* of justification. In this sense it may be said that justification is "received through faith." Conspicuous by its absence is the word *alone.* Rome believes justification is through faith but not through faith alone. Both sides can honestly affirm that justification is received through faith, but only one side can say consistently with its tradition that justification is received through faith alone. To say that justification is received through faith is to affirm something that is "in agreement" with *sola fide,* since *sola fide* also affirms it, but it is not *sola fide* itself because the *sola* is absent.

2. Faith is a gift of God. Reformed theology teaches that the very faith through which we receive justification is the result or product of God's gracious work within us. Since it is the work of God initially, it is seen not as a human achievement but as God's gift.

Rome also teaches that faith is a gift in that it rests on the gracious work of God in and through the sacraments. Though it requires a certain predisposition of the believer and the believer's synergistic cooperation and assent, ultimately it rests on God's grace.

Though *how* faith is wrought in us by God was a matter of dispute between Rome and the Reformation, both parties agreed that it ultimately rests on the initiative of God's grace. A Roman Catholic can say that faith is a gift of God without departing from Catholic orthodoxy. Likewise an Evangelical can affirm the same thing without compromising *sola fide.* When the Roman Catholic and the Evangelical say that faith is a gift of God, they do not have in view the same concept.

3. By our response of faith . . . we enter into the blessings. Again there is agreement as far as it goes, but again the *sola* of *sola fide* is conspicuously absent.

4. Faith is not mere intellectual assent. Martin Luther and John Calvin were accused of easy believism, by which a person can be saved by giving mere intellectual assent to the gospel, a faith that can be construed as a "dead faith" (against which James protested), that yields no works and lacks any volitional or affective element. Against this caricature Luther insisted that true saving faith is a *fides viva,* a living and vital faith that includes more (but not less) than intellectual assent. The historic evangelical definition of saving faith is that it includes content *(notitia),* intellectual assent *(assensus),* and personal trust *(fiducia).* Both Rome and Evangelicalism have always agreed that the faith that justifies is not merely intellectual assent. This point certainly agrees with *sola fide,* but it does not, in itself, give us *sola fide.*

5. Faith is an act of the whole person. That faith involves more than the intellect was never in dispute.

6. Faith results in a changed life. The Reformation formula for *sola fide* was this: Justification is by faith alone, but not by a faith that is alone. Though faith and works can and must be distinguished from one another, they must not be separated. True faith always necessarily and inevitably issues in a changed life, made manifest by works. But the critical point is that these works or changes of life are in no way the *ground* of justification, as they are in the Roman Catholic view. Again we have agreement on certain points, but the historical controversy over the ground of justification is not addressed. In the Reformation view, faith looks outside of itself and beyond itself to the righteousness of Christ as the sole ground of justification. Faith yields the fruit of sanctification, but sanctification flows out of justification and is never its ground.

For the Reformers, faith, distinguished from its fruit, is the instrumental cause of justification, the means by which we subjectively appropriate (via imputation) Christ's objective righteousness. Faith is neither a meritorious cause of justification nor its ground. For Rome the sacraments, chiefly baptism and penance, are the instrumental cause of justification.

The Gift of the Spirit

> [9] In justification we receive the gift of the Holy Spirit, through whom the love of God is poured forth into our hearts (Romans 5:5). The grace of Christ and the gift of the Spirit received through faith (Galatians 3:14) are experienced and expressed in diverse ways by different Christians and in different Christian traditions, but God's gift is never dependent upon our human experience or our ways of expressing that experience.

Paragraph 9 begins, "In justification we receive the gift of the Holy Spirit, through whom the love of God is poured forth into our hearts." This affirmation is remarkably vague and may be a "studied ambiguity," capable of being interpreted in either Roman Catholic or evangelical terms. As stated it poses more problems for Evangelicals than for Catholics.

Both sides agree that justified persons are also indwelt by the Holy Spirit. But the relationship between justification and the indwelling of the Spirit differs radically in the Catholic and evangelical views. The question here is how we understand the phrase "in justification." In the evangelical view the indwelling of the Spirit is a blessing that flows out of justification and that contributes nothing to it. In the Roman view the indwelling of the Spirit helps make a person just, which then becomes the ground of the person's justification. Rome rests the doctrine of justification on the Latin term *iustificare,* which means literally "to make just." Part of the process by which a person is "made just" includes the sanctifying influence of the indwelling Spirit. For the Reformers God declares us just in a legal sense, a declaration that is not based on our sanctification.

The question remains, What is meant by the word *in* in the phrase "in justification"? For Rome the indwelling is contained within the process by which a person is justified. For the Reformers it is a benefit or blessing flowing out of or resulting *from* justification. The wording of this paragraph is sufficiently vague to allow for either view.

That this affirmation may have been intentionally ambiguous is indicated by the following words expressing diversity in experience or expression: "The grace of Christ and the gift of the Spirit received through faith (Galatians 3:14) are experienced and expressed in diverse ways by different Christians and in different Christian traditions, but God's gift is never dependent upon our human experience or our ways of expressing that experience."

The Body of Christ

> [10] While faith is inherently personal, it is not a purely private possession but involves participation in the body of Christ. By baptism we are visibly incorporated into the community of faith and committed to a life of discipleship. "We were buried therefore with him by baptism into death, so that as Christ was raised from the dead by the glory of the Father, we too might walk in newness of life" (Romans 6:4).

A similar problem of ambiguity attends paragraph 10 concerning baptism. It asserts, "By baptism we are visibly incorporated into the community of faith and committed to a life of discipleship." What is left undiscussed here is the question of baptism's efficacy and its relationship to faith. The Roman view of baptismal regeneration and its *ex opere operato* efficacy was affirmed at the Council of Trent: "If anyone says that by the sacraments of the New Law grace is not conferred *ex opere operato,* but that faith alone in the divine promise is sufficient to obtain grace, let him be anathema."[1]

Again this statement can be interpreted in such a way as to accommodate either the Roman Catholic or the Reformation view of baptism and does nothing to address the historical controversy on this matter, despite the fact that this controversy touches heavily on the issue of *sola fide.*

The Life of Holiness

> [11] By their faith and baptism, Christians are bound to live according to the law of love in obedience to Jesus Christ the Lord. Scripture calls this the life of holiness, or sanctification. "Since we have these promises, dear friends, let us purify ourselves from everything that contaminates body and spirit, perfecting holiness out of reverence for God" (2 Corinthians 7:1). Sanctification is not fully accomplished at the beginning of our life in Christ, but is progressively furthered as we struggle, with God's grace and help, against adversity and temptation. In this struggle we are assured that Christ's grace will be sufficient for us, enabling us to persevere to the end. When we fail, we can still turn to God in humble repentance and confidently ask for, and receive, his forgiveness.

Paragraph 11 speaks of the progress of sanctification. It affirms that our "sanctification is not fully accomplished at the beginning of our life in Christ, but is progressively furthered." Again this affirmation can be adopted to accommodate either the Roman Catholic or the Reformation view. For the Reformers justification is followed by progressive sanctification. For Rome sanctification precedes justification, and the grace of justification (which is integral to our "life in Christ") can be augmented or diminished. Remember that according to Rome God will not declare a person just unless or until that person is inherently just. This goal is reached progressively as one cooperates with infused grace.

An Assured Hope

> [12] We may therefore have assured hope for the eternal life promised to us in Christ. As we have shared in his sufferings, we will share in his

final glory. "We shall be like him, for we shall see him as he is" (1 John 3:2). While we dare not presume upon the grace of God, the promise of God in Christ is utterly reliable, and faith in that promise overcomes anxiety about our eternal future. We are bound by faith itself to have firm hope, to encourage one another in that hope, and in such hope we rejoice. For believers "through faith are shielded by God's power until the coming of the salvation to be revealed in the last time" (1 Peter 1:5).

This paragraph raises questions regarding our assurance of salvation. Historical Reformation theology embraces the doctrine that the believer, trusting in God's promises, may have assurance of salvation. Catholic theology, on the other hand, has a different view of assurance. The Council of Trent, in a chapter entitled "Against the Vain Confidence of Heretics," declared: ". . . no one can know with the certainty of faith, which cannot be subject to error, that he has obtained the grace of God."[2] In a later chapter the council declared that one cannot know he is numbered among the elect "except by special revelation."[3] Rome has consistently denied that we can have assurance of salvation except by special revelation.

Yet paragraph 12 of GOS declares: "We may therefore have assured hope for the eternal life promised to us in Christ." Have the Roman Catholic participants here departed from Catholic orthodoxy? Not necessarily. What is affirmed is the possibility of an "assured hope." Is an assured hope the same thing as assurance? On the surface it would seem so since a hope that is assured would mean assurance. The phrase "assured hope" may, however, mean a firm or strong "hope" (in the sense of desire) without actual assurance of the outcome. For example, when someone asks me if I think the Pittsburgh Steelers will win their next game, I may reply "I sure hope so." This is not the same thing as having assurance they will win. It simply indicates that I am certain about what I desire or hope the outcome will be.

The Gift of Salvation: Part 3

13. As justified sinners we have been saved, we are being saved, and we will be saved.
14. As believers we are sent into the world and commissioned to be bearers of the good news.
15. We commit ourselves to evangelizing everyone.
16. We defend religious freedom for all.
17. We must not allow our witness as Christians to be compromised by half-hearted discipleship or needlessly divisive disputes.
18. All who truly believe in Jesus Christ are brothers and sisters in the Lord and must not allow their differences, however important, to undermine this great truth.
19. We affirm our unity in the gospel.

5

Divisive Disputes and Legitimate Questions

From assurance *The Gift of Salvation* moves to evangelism and several less controversial paragraphs.

Bearers of the Good News

[13] Thus it is that as justified sinners we have been saved, we are being saved, and we will be saved. All this is the gift of God. Faith issues in a confident hope for a new heaven and a new earth in which God's creating and redeeming purposes are gloriously fulfilled. "Therefore God has highly exalted him and bestowed on him the name which is above every name, that at the name of Jesus every knee should bow, in heaven and on earth and under the earth, and every tongue confess that Jesus Christ is Lord, to the glory of God the Father" (Philippians 2:9–11).

[14] As believers we are sent into the world and commissioned to be bearers of the good news, to serve one another in love, to do good to all, and to evangelize everyone everywhere. It is our responsibility and firm resolve to bring to the whole world the tidings of God's love and of the salvation accomplished in our crucified, risen, and returning Lord. Many are in grave peril of being eternally lost because they do not know the way to salvation.

[15] In obedience to the Great Commission of our Lord, we commit ourselves to evangelizing everyone. We must share the fullness of God's saving truth with all, including members of our several communities. Evangelicals must speak the gospel to Catholics and Catholics to Evangelicals, always speaking the truth in love, so that "working hard to maintain the unity of the Spirit in the bond of peace . . . the body of Christ may be built up until we all reach unity in the faith and in the knowledge of the Son of God" (Ephesians 4:3, 12–13).

[16] Moreover, we defend religious freedom for all. Such freedom is grounded in the dignity of the human person created in the image of God and must be protected also in civil law.

While paragraphs 13 through 16 offer no substantive problems, paragraph 17 is the most problematic of the entire document.

Needlessly Divisive Disputes

[17] We must not allow our witness as Christians to be compromised by half-hearted discipleship or needlessly divisive disputes. While we rejoice in the unity we have discovered and are confident of the fundamental truths about the gift of salvation we have affirmed, we recognize that there are necessarily interrelated questions that require further and urgent exploration. Among such questions are these: the meaning of baptismal regeneration, the Eucharist, and sacramental grace; the historic uses of the language of justification as it relates to imputed and transformative righteousness; the normative status of justification in relation to all Christian doctrine; the assertion that while justification is by faith alone, the faith that receives salvation is never alone; diverse understandings of merit, reward, purgatory, and indulgences; Marian devotion and the assistance of the saints in the life of salvation; and the possibility of salvation for those who have not been evangelized.

[18] On these and other questions, we recognize that there are also some differences within both the Evangelical and Catholic communities. We are committed to examining these questions further in our continuing conversations. All who truly believe in Jesus Christ are brothers and sisters in the Lord and must not allow their differences, however important, to undermine this great truth, or to deflect them from bearing witness together to God's gift of salvation in Christ. "I appeal to you, brothers, in the name of our Lord Jesus Christ, that all of you agree with one another so that there may be no divisions among you and that you may be perfectly united in mind and thought" (1 Corinthians 1:10).

Paragraph 17 begins with the admonition, "We must not allow our witness as Christians to be compromised by half-hearted discipleship or needlessly divisive disputes." Throughout its history the church has certainly seen a host of disputes that proved to be needlessly divisive. One reason for disputes is that Christians take truth so seriously. All too often, however, disputes over minor points escalate into bitter controversies that say more about our pride than our humility.

The problem with the opening sentence of paragraph 17 is not that it seeks to discourage needlessly divisive disputes, but that it begins a paragraph that then lists questions "that require further and urgent exploration." If this lead sentence serves as a thematic statement for the entire paragraph, it lends credence to the inference that the issues listed for further discussion are also "needlessly divisive." Since the document *already* affirms a uniting of faith while leaving these matters on the table, it would seem that, while they still require "urgent" exploration, these matters should not divide us. Otherwise they would compromise the unity that has already been affirmed.

When asked what this first sentence means, Timothy George, Thomas C. Oden, and J. I. Packer responded in a letter to *Christianity Today* with the following explanation:

> When *The Gift of Salvation* speaks of "needlessly divisive disputes" between Roman Catholics and evangelicals, it does not refer to the many weighty theological matters on which we still conscientiously disagree, such as sacramental theology, Marian devotion, purgatory, and so forth. *The Gift of Salvation* takes note of

> *these* matters, referring to them as "serious and persistent differences" which are "necessarily interrelated" with the affirmations we have made in common, and are thus future agenda items for us. The fact that these issues are "on the table" does not mean that they are "up for grabs," but rather that they must be pursued with rigor and honesty in our continuing dialogue. By "needlessly divisive disputes" we mean the kind of mutual recrimination and uncharitable taunting that has resulted in Protestant-bashing and Catholic-baiting in the past and that still persists today.[1]

According to at least three participants in GOS, then, the initial sentence of paragraph 17 does not serve as a thematic statement and therefore one should *not* infer that the issues still on the table are needlessly divisive. Though we are indeed grateful for this clarification, it nevertheless leaves us with two problems.

The first problem is the infelicitous use of language in the phrase "needlessly divisive disputes." Ordinarily in theological controversy, the term *dispute* refers to doctrinal debates, not to personal recriminations or uncharitable taunting. This is at least a literary flaw in a document in which we would have hoped for and expected more articulate expression. If this is what the document's authors meant, they should have said it in the first place. Lest I be guilty of uncharitable taunting, however, let me say that any document so constructed is vulnerable at points to infelicitous language that lends itself to misunderstanding. Since the letter clarifies the authors' intent, charity demands that we accept their explanation as it stands.

The second problem is far more serious. If these "weighty theological matters" remain on the table for future discussion, then they were *not resolved* before unity was achieved. No matter then how weighty, serious, or urgent these matters are, they are obviously not weighty, serious, or urgent enough to preclude the unity of faith declared in GOS. Whatever the literary intent or function of the opening sentence, we must still conclude that since these matters are not yet resolved and since unity has already been declared, then these matters must be deemed to be "needlessly divisive" no matter their actual gravity.

This poses the greatest problem of GOS, and it is what I and many others consider its fatal flaw. Some of the issues, especially some not explicitly mentioned in the letter to *Christianity Today* but presumably included in the letter's "and so forth," go directly to the heart of the Reformation controversy over *sola fide*. For example, the normative status of justification and the language of imputation were central to the historic and most divisive dispute in Christian history, and the magisterial Reformers would hardly have subsumed them under an "and so forth."

Legitmate Questions

The rest of paragraph 17 mentions specific matters that are included in the "interrelated questions that require further and urgent exploration." These include the following:

1. The meaning of baptismal regeneration
2. The eucharist
3. Sacramental grace
4. The language of justification
5. The normative status of the doctrine of justification
6. The assertion that the faith that receives salvation is never alone
7. Merit, reward, purgatory, and indulgences
8. Marian devotion
9. The assistance of the saints
10. Salvation for the unevangelized

This list is somewhat lengthy, and a full discussion of each point would require a large book or several books to analyze. In the space below we will limit our analysis to the most critical points on the list.

1. The meaning of baptismal regeneration. The Roman Catholic Church is not alone in affirming baptismal regeneration. This doctrine is found in some Protestant bodies, especially in historic Lutheranism. Technical differences appear with respect to the scope and meaning of regeneration. But one crucial matter is involved: the relationship of baptism to justification. Rome clearly affirms that baptism is the instrumental cause of justification, the sacramental means by which the grace of justification is infused into the soul. Emphatically rejecting this view, the Reformers insisted that the instrumental cause of justification is faith and faith alone. If the issue of justification's instrumental cause remains "on the table," then we conclude that the doctrine of *sola fide* remains on the table. This confirms what was stated earlier, that though GOS affirms certain elements of *sola fide,* it does not affirm *sola fide* itself.

2. The eucharist. The doctrine of eucharist includes transubstantiation and the idea of the sacrifice (albeit "unbloody") of Christ being repeated in the mass. This doctrine sharply divides Roman Catholics and Evangelicals and raises serious matters of Christology. It does not, however, go to the heart of the doctrine of *sola fide* except as it relates to the once-for-all nature and sufficiency of Christ's atonement. The Council of Trent anathematized those who deny transubstantiation.[2] This council also declared: "If anyone says that in the mass a true and real sacrifice is not offered to God; or that to be offered is nothing else than that Christ is given to us to eat, let him be anathema."[3] Here we see that Rome considered these matters as necessarily dividing.

3. Sacramental grace. Both Catholics and Evangelicals believe that in some sense the sacraments are "means of grace," but they differ on the nature of grace itself and how it is conferred. This touches heavily on *sola fide* again because in the Roman view the grace of justification is infused sacramentally and sacerdotally, whereas in the evangelical view the grace of justification is conferred by faith.

4. The language of justification. GOS does not say that what remains on the table for further and urgent discussion is the question of the ground of justification, the imputation of Christ's righteousness versus the inherent righteousness gained via infusion. What remains on the table is instead "the historic uses of the language of justification" as it relates to these questions.

This could mean that GOS participants have already agreed in principle on the *concept* or *nature* of justification, but have not yet agreed on the proper language to express these things. Thus the only serious matter left to discuss regarding justification is a linguistic one.

In trying to discern what the Roman Catholic participants in GOS mean by this, knowing that I cannot read their minds, I can only speculate. One thing that immediately comes to mind is an appeal that has been made frequently in the twentieth century by Roman Catholics who have embraced the so-called "new theology" of their church's progressive party (found largely in the Church's Western wing as distinguished from its Latin wing), an appeal that has provoked serious, and at times bitter, controversy within the Roman communion.

This appeal is that while doctrinal substance does not change, doctrinal formulations do. In the controversy of the 1960s over the formulation of the doctrine of the Lord's Supper, men like Edward Schillebeeckx wanted to change the formulation of "transubstantiation" to "transignification." This resulted in the encyclical *Mysterium fidei* (1965),[4] in which Pope Paul VI ruled that neither the doctrine nor its formulation is subject to change.

The doctrine of infallibility always lurks in the background. If the change in formulation involves an actual change in the doctrine's meaning or substance, by way of correction, it would be tantamount to acknowledging error in a doctrine that has been defined "infallibly" by the church. In this case not only would an error in doctrine be admitted, but infallibility would be repudiated as well.

Perhaps what GOS means then is that where there previously was a serious misunderstanding of each other's doctrine of justification, now the Roman Catholic and Evangelical participants in GOS have cleared up that misunderstanding at least among themselves. What is left to do is to clear up the linguistic confusion that has borne this misunderstanding for almost five centuries. That is, the two sides have believed the same thing all along, but have expressed it in different ways.

What else could paragraph 17 mean? Perhaps it means that real agreement in substance has been reached and that this agreement is the result of movement by either side or both. That is, the new agreement has been reached because (1) the Roman Catholic participants have abandoned their church's historic view and embraced the evangelical view, (2) the evangelical participants have abandoned the historic evangelical view, or (3) both sides have abandoned their historic views to meet somewhere in the middle.

There remains one more possibility, which in my judgment is the most likely: The two sides have reached agreement on certain elements of what the Reformers meant by *sola fide,* but other elements of *sola fide* have not yet been resolved. As I have already labored to show, those elements of *sola fide* about which agreement is affirmed were never in dispute. It is the crucial disputed elements of *sola fide* that remain on the table. If this is the case, then the announcement of agreement is somewhat premature. Though some steps of clarification have been reached regarding points on which agreement had always existed, nobody, especially the Roman Catholics, has changed his historic view.

It seems that if the historic language of justification, particularly as it relates to imputation versus transformative grace (real infusion), is still on the table, then the content and meaning of that language remain on the table as well. The Reformers were not so inarticulate as to fail to express adequately the difference between imputed righteousness and infused or inherent righteousness. If the language of imputation remains on the table, I suspect it is because the doctrine of imputation remains on the table. If that is the case, then we must conclude *non cornutum* ("without horns") that *sola fide* remains on the table.

If imputation is essential to *sola fide* and *sola fide* is essential to the gospel, then manifestly, as long as the doctrine of imputation remains on the table, the gospel lies there with it. In this case the two parties have not reached an agreement on the essentials of the gospel itself.

In a later letter of clarification, some evangelical participants with whom I was in dialogue declared that agreement had been reached on the "basic dimensions" of the gospel. It is true that some basic dimensions have been agreed on, but they are the basic dimensions that have always been agreed on. The gospel itself has not been agreed on, and the locus of the disagreement is of the essence of the gospel.

5. The normative status of the doctrine of justification. That the doctrine of *sola fide* was considered normative for Christian faith by the Reformers of the sixteenth century is clear. Martin Luther spoke of *sola fide* as the article on which the church stands or falls. John Calvin described it as the hinge on which everything turns. Likewise, J. I. Packer used the metaphor of Atlas holding up the world to illustrate the function *sola fide* plays in the Christian faith.[5]

A recent issue of the *Lutheran Quarterly* reported on criticisms leveled against the *Joint Declaration on the Doctrine of Justification* by some German Lutherans. One of their chief reasons for rejecting the *Joint Declaration* is that "the doctrine of justification has to do with the basis and the whole of Christian truth."[6] Here these German theologians reaffirm the thesis that *sola fide* is the article on which the church stands or falls.

In GOS the normative role of *sola fide* is one of the issues left on the table. If the GOS did reach an accord on justification, it certainly is clear that GOS does not affrim the normativity of justification. Though it explicitly remains on the table for future consideration, implicitly and *de facto* it has already been rejected. If Evangelicals are willing to declare a common faith and mission and a unity in the gospel before resolving the question of the normativity of *sola fide,* this can only mean that what remains to be discussed about *sola fide,* especially with respect to imputation, is not normative. This indicates that the points of agreement that have already been reached are sufficient to satisfy the matter of normativity. Evangelicals who signed GOS could still affirm the normativity of a doctrine of justification, but not the normativity of the doctrine of *sola fide,* which clearly contains the essential ingredient of imputation.

6. The assertion that the faith that receives salvation is never alone. The inclusion of this assertion on the list of matters requiring further discussion reinforces the fact that the *sola* of *sola fide* has not been resolved by the participants. The magisterial Reformers themselves affirmed that justification is by faith alone but not by a faith that is alone. The Reformers were declaring that saving faith, the only instrument of justification, is not a dead or empty faith. Luther insisted that saving faith is a *fides* *viva,* a "living" or "vital" faith. This is reflected in the Epistle of James, which emphasizes that faith without works is dead (James 2:17). For the Reformers a true faith, the faith that justifies, is always attended by good works. True faith always *necessarily, inevitably,* and *immediately* yields the fruit of obedience. Without works the faith that is professed is not true faith. Here faith and works are (and must be) *distinguished* but are not (and must not be) *separated.*

Though the Reformers declared that faith always yields the fruit of works, they insisted that the works flowing out of faith are in no way justification's ground. This is consistent with their view of faith, which also is not the ground of justification but is the instrument by which the sinner grabs hold of and appropriates the imputed righteousness of Christ. This imputed righteousness is the sole ground of our justification. Not by works do we gain the merit of Christ, but by faith alone. In this regard works contribute nothing to our justification. They remain the *fruit* of justification and belong to sanctification. In the Reformation view sanctification follows justification, while in the Roman view sanctification precedes justification and is its ground.

That the relationship of faith to its subsequent fruit remains on the table illustrates once again that what GOS has affirmed about justification falls short of *sola fide.* Until the relationship of faith and works to justification is settled, there can be no genuine agreement on the doctrine of justification.

7. Merit, reward, purgatory, and indulgences. To acknowledge that issues of merit and reward are not yet resolved is to concede that, whatever else GOS has achieved, it has not reconciled the chief issues of the Reformation. We have already seen that Rome has always talked about a kind of "gracious merit" that is not strict merit, but is nevertheless true merit, even if it is limited to "congruous" merit. The Reformers rejected all human merit (including congruous merit) in justification, and they viewed the justified sinner as possessing in himself only demerit. The rewards given to believers in heaven are at best what Augustine describes as "God's crowning his own gifts." Though God promises such rewards to the faithful, it is not because they have earned these rewards. Our best works are only "splendid vices," which place no moral obligation on God to reward them.

Included in the questions for further exploration is a reference to purgatory and indulgences. Again, as long as purgatory remains on the table, there can be no agreement on *sola fide.* The notion of purgatory is utterly and completely incompatible with *sola fide.* If the believer must be purified or purged of all remaining impurity before entering heaven, then the sufficiency and efficacy of the merit of Christ for our salvation are nullified.

Jesuit scholar and GOS signatory Avery Dulles is quoted by *World* as saying he sees no inconsistency between justification by faith alone and purgatory: "All those people in purgatory already have been justified by faith; now they are being cleansed and serving their time."[7]

This quote, if accurate, reveals the on-going conflict between Rome and the Reformation. If Dulles is affirming justification by faith alone *(sola fide),* it is not the *sola fide* of the Reformation. The Protestant doctrine of *sola fide* leaves no room for purgatory or for justified believers "serving time" before entering into the glory of heaven. If purgatory and indulgences remain possible affirmations of faith, then whatever was jointly agreed on was not the gospel of *sola fide.*

8–10. Marian devotion, the assistance of the saints, and salvation for the unevangelized. The role of Mary in the life of the church is a point of dispute not only between Protestants and Catholics but also between Catholic "minimalists" and Catholic "maximalists." The maximalists have lobbied to have Mary declared coredemptrix with Jesus, but this has not yet become dogma. The assistance of Mary and the saints does come into play, however, with respect to the treasury of merit, which was denounced by the Reformers and has been reaffirmed by Rome as recently as the *Catechism of the Catholic Church* (1994).[8] Here the works of supererogation performed by Mary and the saints are added to the merit of Christ and can be dispensed by the church, exercising her "power of the keys" to those lacking in merit.

These matters cloud the issue of imputation and the righteousness and merit of Christ being the sole ground of our justification. For the Reformers the only merit available to us for salvation is the merit of Christ. That merit is perfect and sufficient for our salvation; it is not open to augmentation or diminution. As long as this matter remains unresolved, we cannot have agreement on the point that our justification is grounded in the imputation of the righteousness of Christ alone.

These matters for "further discussion" indicate how deeply divided the historic Roman Catholic and evangelical views of salvation really are. The differences are systemic, not partial; they are radical, not slight.

Unity in the Truth?

> [19] As Evangelicals who thank God for the heritage of the Reformation and affirm with conviction its classic confessions, as Catholics who are conscientiously faithful to the teaching of the Catholic Church, and as disciples together of the Lord Jesus Christ who recognize our debt to our Christian forebears and our obligations to our contemporaries and those who will come after us, we affirm our unity in the gospel that we have here professed. In our continuing discussions, we seek no unity other than unity in the truth. Only unity in the truth can be pleasing to the Lord and Savior whom we together serve, for he is "the way, the truth, and the life" (John 14:6).

Perhaps no section of GOS is more troublesome to me than this closing paragraph. Here is a solemn declaration of unity in the gospel, codiscipleship of Christ, and a unity of service to him. At the same time the Evangelicals affirm "with conviction" the classic confessions of the Reformation, and the Catholics say they are "conscientiously faithful" to the teaching of the Catholic Church.

What? Is convicted adherence to the classic confessions of the Reformation compatible with conscientious fidelity to the teaching of the Roman Catholic Church? Was the entire Reformation struggle for the biblical gospel a colossal misunderstanding?

Neither side grants that they have departed from their historic positions. Does this not indicate then that either there are no real historic differences in their understanding of the gospel or that the differences are not so serious as to preclude a unity in the gospel?

Both sides have labored the point that real differences do exist and have existed for centuries. The *Christianity Today* letter cited earlier quotes Cardinal Edward Cassidy: "This does not mean that evangelicals and Catholics have overcome all their doctrinal differences or that their understanding of the gospel and of the Christian message has suddenly become identical. We will surely continue to evangelize according to our beliefs."[9]

Cassidy indicates that real differences do in fact exist. We are left to conclude that whatever differences exist between the evangelical and Catholic signatories, these differences pose no barrier to unity in the gospel. We must also conclude that the signatories agree that whatever differences exist between classical Reformation theology and orthodox Roman Catholicism, they do not nullify a real unity of the gospel.

Timothy George heralded the achievement of GOS because, for one reason, it indicates a "movement toward a Reformation understanding of some issues."[10] We ask where that movement is if the Catholic signatories declare their conscientious fidelity to the teaching of Rome.

As reported in *Christianity Today,* James M. Boice declared at a Washington, D.C., meeting in February 1998 that GOS "sells out the Reformation."[11] A sell-out is a form of betrayal. This is the emotional side of the issue. Evangelicals who have earnestly contended for the evangelical gospel have felt betrayed by the ECT initiative, leaving a serious rupture among Evangelicals, a rupture in desperate need of healing. This need is what prompted the careful work of the Committee for Evangelical Unity in the Gospel, which produced the document we shall explore in part 3.

In the lead article of a recent issue of *Proclaiming the Gospel,* the editor, Michael P. Gendron, states:

> The creators of the GOS document may want us to believe they are affirming "justification by faith alone." However, they are merely affirming a "misrepresentation" of what the Reformers meant by "justification by faith alone." The Reformers were never so careless as to limit the definition to "the gift of justification is

> received through faith," as GOS proposes. The Reformers knew that Catholic theologians could affirm language like that and still miss the Gospel. If we choose to be ambiguous on the doctrine of justification, then we end up with a gospel that anyone can embrace, a gospel void of the power of God to save. . . .
>
> . . . The gospel which they have professed is neither the Gospel of grace nor the gospel of Rome. It is a gospel of ecumenical unity that will only bring a deeper division within the evangelical church.[12]

If we are concerned about unity in the gospel, we must first make evangelical unity a top priority. The broader we seek to make that unity, the less unity there is among Evangelicals themselves. This is the downside of ecumenism.

The Problem of Studied Ambiguity

Perhaps the greatest weakness of ecumenism is its tendency to use studied ambiguities as a means to achieve unity. But such unity must, of necessity, be hollow, because it dodges issues by using evasive language.

When GOS was released, one participant stated he was glad it contains very few intentional ambiguities. If there are "few," then surely there are some. The presence of even one studied ambiguity, if it appears at a crucial point, can wreck true agreement.

The twentieth century has produced a spirit of urgency with respect to clarity in theological discourse. Two world wars, the rise of nihilism, and the pervasive influence of philosophical and ethical relativism have raised the stakes on the pursuit of truth. The basic question of "meaning" has been applied, not only to words (as in the God-talk controversy), but also to the meaning of life itself.

The ecumenical movement has sought ways to transcend the confusion and separation that a multitude of schisms have left us with. The split between liberal and conservative has affected virtually every Christian denomination.

To heal these splits we have seen renewed interest in creedal statements: their meaning, purpose, and value. The concern to reformulate doctrinal statements has been integral to much Protestant-Catholic dialogue in the past. Any honest dialogue must begin with a clear and precise formulation of the issues or problems under discussion. Precise identification of a problem is crucial to solving it. The lack of understanding between opposing parties is not all that separates them, but it often is a major contributing factor.

The first step then is to gain a clear and precise understanding of the differences between opposing parties. Without that the parties will tend to speak past each other rather than to and with each other. They will also tend to minimize those differences and even succumb to relativism, which carries in its wake religious skepticism.

In his book *Vatikaans Concilie en Nieuwe Theologie*, G. C. Berkouwer cogently analyzes twentieth-century developments in Rome. Discussing what the modern Roman Catholic Church means by the immutability of doctrine, he says: "When Rome speaks of immutability, she means that the truth of the dogma remains constant. This, however, is not a negation of historical influences in the formulation of the dogma. Historical influences are obvious in the cases of Galileo, Quesnel, and the gradual change in the church's view of evolution. Such developments come as new applications for contemporary times."[13]

Here, as noted earlier, it is necessary to distinguish between reformulation and relativization. The postmodern method "corrects" doctrine by relativizing it. It is one thing to reformulate doctrine to make it more intelligible to a new generation of people; it is another to change the doctrine surreptitiously by casting it in different language. Legitimate reformulation seeks merely to *clarify* by new forms that retain the *original intent* of the old formulas.

Hans Küng addresses this matter in *Kerk in Concilie:*

> One dogma can be living in various formulations. The one joyous message of Christ is given in four different Gospels. The Christian faith has an historical character which is expressed in continuous

> new formulations. Many attempts have been made to unite all men under one creedal formulation, but it becomes more and more evident that no single formula can completely exhaust the content of the faith in its entirety. The faith can be the same as the formulations differ. Behind the various confessions stand physiological, esthetic, philological, logical, historical, ethnological, philosophical and religious presuppositions; different individual and collective experiences, languages and world-views, world-structures, and human concepts; various traditions of particular people, theological schools, etc.[14]

Küng cites another crucial result of imprecise expression: "Often it occurs that one sees, in the expressions of another, only what is lacking or, on the other hand, in one's own only what is there. Also it occurs that one sees in his own formulation the content of truth, and in the other, the lack of truth."[15]

Here Küng understands the polemical character of much doctrinal formulation. Integral to each creed are the historical circumstances in which it was first expressed. The most powerful driving force for creedal statements in history has been the threat of heresy. In every age the church has been forced to clarify its own faith to distinguish and differentiate it from the views of heretics. This was true at Nicea, Chalcedon, and virtually every ecumenical council.

Küng, in noting the historical context of theological formulations, does not conclude that such factors plead for ambiguity to allow room for wider meaning. On the contrary—because of the historical and polemical contexts in which doctrine has been formulated—it is all the more imperative to achieve the greatest precision possible. Imprecision, especially when intentional, does not resolve conflict. It merely seeks to mask it through the use of studied ambiguity and to provide a formula for dishonest "agreement."

This problem was encountered in the sixteenth century when earnest attempts were made to resolve the Reformation controversy. Most notable were efforts undertaken at Regensburg.

Regensburg Redux

In April 1541 Charles V, emperor of the Holy Roman Empire, convened a theological conference at Regensburg (sometimes referred to as Ratisbon). He sought to unify his empire against threats from the outside.

This was not the first effort to heal the breach between Rome and the Reformers. Erasmus of Rotterdam had written *On Establishing Concord in the Church* (1533), in which he sought a middle ground for reconciliation. Also a provincial council was held in 1536 in an effort to bring reform to the Roman Church. Other conferences were held at Hagenau (1540) and Worms (1541), but both ended in failure.

At Regensburg the emperor appointed three representatives from each side. Protestants were represented by Philipp Melanchthon, Martin Bucer, and Johann Pistorius (John Calvin was present as an observer). Roman Catholics were represented by Johann Eck (Eckius), Johann Gropper, and Julius Pflug (Cardinal Gasparo Contarini represented Pope Paul III). In the initial stages of the meeting, much agreement was reached that seemed to signal a willingness on both sides to reach common ground on the doctrine of justification. This agreement was subject to the approval of the Diet, which was not forthcoming. James Buchanan says of this event:

> ... it throws an instructive light on the new policy which began to be adopted at that time by the adherents of Rome, and which has been pursued, more or less consistently, ever since, we may mark, *first,* the large concessions which were now made in favour of the Protestant doctrine of Justification; and, *secondly,* the careful reservation of one point, and only one, which was so ambiguously expressed as to be susceptible of different interpretations, while, according to the sense in which it was understood, it involved the whole difference between the Popish, and the Protestant, method of acceptance with God—between Justification by imputed, and Justification by infused or inherent, righteousness.[16]

Once the agreement's ambiguities were exposed, it was openly denounced by both parties. The papal representative, Cardinal Contarini, was charged by Cardinal Caraffa (who later became Pope Paul IV) with betraying the cause of the Church on the issue of justification.[17]

The irenic-spirited Melanchthon was unusually harsh in his complaint against Eck, charging him with "sophisms and juggling tricks." Melanchthon said: "He sports with terms of the most serious import—continually conceals his real meaning, and only aims to embarrass an adversary. There is great danger in encountering sycophants of this kind."[18]

Buchanan provides a lengthy but helpful warning to the church: "We learn another lesson from what occurred at the Diet of Ratisbon [Regensburg]. It shows the possibility of appearing to concede almost everything, while one point is reserved, or wrapped up in ambiguous language, which is found afterwards sufficient to neutralize every concession, and to leave the parties as much at variance as before. It has been justly said that, in controversies of faith, the difference between antagonist systems is often reduced to a line sharp as a razor's edge, yet on one side of that line there is God's truth, and on the other a departure from it."[19]

Buchanan continues: "At Ratisbon, the difference between the Popish and Protestant doctrines of Justification seemed to resolve itself into one point, and even on that point both parties held some views in common. It might seem, then, that there was no radical or irreconcilable difference between the two; and yet, when they came to explain their respective views, it was found that they were contending for two opposite methods of Justification—the one by an inherent, the other by an imputed, righteousness. . . ."[20]

Buchanan concludes with a warning to future generations of evangelical Protestants:

> This fact shows the utter folly of every attempt to reconcile two systems, which are radically opposed, by means of a compromise between them; and the great danger of engaging in private conferences with a view to that end. In the open field of controversy,

truth, so far from being endangered, is ventilated, cleared, and defined; in the secret conclaves of divines, and the cabinets of princes, it is often smothered, or silenced. It has far less to fear from discussion, than from diplomacy. There can be no honest compromise between the Popish and the Protestant doctrine[s] of Justification—the one is at direct variance with the other, not in respect of verbal expression merely, but in respect of their fundamental principles—and any settlement, on the basis of mutual concession, could only be made by means of ambiguous expressions, and could amount to nothing more than a hollow truce, liable to be broken by either party as soon as the subject was brought again into serious discussion. This was the abortive result of the apparent agreement at Ratisbon; it settled no question—it satisfied no party—and it led afterwards to much misunderstanding and mutual recrimination.[21]

In an article in *Modern Reformation,* R. Scott Clark, academic dean and church historian at Westminster Seminary in California, makes a detailed comparison between the Regensburg doctrine of justification and GOS. He notes that at Regensburg a concept of "double justice" *(duplex iustitia)* was introduced by Johann Gropper. Gropper taught that one is justified by an infusion of divine justice *(iustitia inhaerens)* which leads to the addition of more justice through sanctification *(iustitia acquisita).* Clark writes:

> The "double justice" scheme of Regensburg has not gone away quietly. It has become the model for ARCIC (1987) and ECT II (1997). . . .
>
> Thus with ECT II, we have come full circle to Regensburg and Cardinal Contarini's doctrine of double justice. It was one thing, however, for Melanchthon, Bucer, and Calvin to treat Regensburg as a victory over Rome in the 1540s. It is quite something else for evangelicals to try that trick again 450 years later. With Luther we too ought vigorously to reject this version of double justice. Protestants cannot subscribe to a statement on justification which makes even divinely, graciously worked sanctification any part of the ground of our justification. Sanctification is and must be the fruit of justification. Here we must stand, we can do no other.[22]

Part 3

The Gospel of Jesus Christ: An Explanation

6

Unity in the Gospel

In the aftermath of *The Gift of Salvation,* a major issue developed between the Evangelicals who signed the document and those who opposed it. Speaking as one who opposed the document, I voiced my concern that both ECT and GOS could provoke, and already had provoked, a serious disruption in a long-standing evangelical unity. I raised this question: "If some Evangelicals declare a unity in the gospel with their Roman Catholic cosigners and other Evangelicals deny such a unity, do the two disagreeing groups of Evangelicals have unity in the gospel with each other?" To state it another way: If I do not have a unity in the gospel with Rome and other Evangelicals declare that they do, can I still have a unity in the gospel with them?

At first glance it may appear that if the Roman Catholic view of the gospel is antithetical to the evangelical view, then any professing Evangelical who declares unity in the gospel with Rome is no longer an Evangelical and I can have no unity in the gospel with them.

If evangelical signatories of ECT and GOS actually embraced the Roman Catholic view of justification, and if they knowingly and willingly repudiated the evangelical doctrine of justification, then, manifestly, I could not declare my unity in the gospel with them. But I do not think for a minute that the evangelical signatories did this. I have spoken at length with many if not most of them, and to a man they have emphatically declared their adherence to *sola fide*. They are convinced that their Roman Catholic counterparts are the ones who have moved, now embracing key aspects of the Reformation view. Though I disagree with the Evangelicals' assessment of what these initiatives achieved, I remain confident that these men intended to be faithful to *sola fide*.

But the cloud of controversy hanging over the ECT initiatives creates an urgent need for Evangelicals to reaffirm together their commitment to the historic evangelical doctrine of *sola fide*. Regardless of what Rome does, it is imperative that gospel unity among Evangelicals not be destroyed.

A team of Evangelicals representing both those who signed GOS and those who opposed it, after discussing the situation, agreed to construct a statement on unity in the gospel that could help to restore and strengthen historic evangelical unity. I have been involved with the drafting committee from the beginning. The group framed an opening statement of commitment to historic Evangelicalism, followed by a series of affirmations and denials with respect to the biblical gospel. What follows in part 3 of this book is a commentary on these articles of affirmation and denial. The affirmation-and-denial format was used to avoid any ambiguity, making it clear not only what is meant but also what is not meant.

Of course no doctrinal statement or creed can be written so tightly that no unscrupulous person can subscribe to it with fingers crossed and meanings twisted. We trust, however, that this will not be the case among earnest Evangelicals.

Before looking at the articles of affirmation and denial, it is necessary to read the full text of *The Gospel of Jesus Christ: An Evangelical Celebration*.

† † † † † † † † † † † † †

The Gospel of Jesus Christ: An Evangelical Celebration

For God so loved the world that he gave his one and only Son, that whoever believes in him shall not perish but have eternal life (John 3:16).

Sing to the Lord, for he has done glorious things; let this be known to all the world (Isaiah 12:5).

Preamble

The Gospel of Jesus Christ is news, good news: the best and most important news that any human being ever hears.

This Gospel declares the only way to know God in peace, love, and joy is through the reconciling death of Jesus Christ the risen Lord.

This Gospel is the central message of the Holy Scriptures, and is the true key to understanding them.

This Gospel identifies Jesus Christ, the Messiah of Israel, as the Son of God and God the Son, the second Person of the Holy Trinity, whose incarnation, ministry, death, resurrection, and ascension fulfilled the Father's saving will. His death for sins and his resurrection from the dead were promised beforehand by the prophets and attested by eyewitnesses. In God's own time and in God's own way, Jesus Christ shall return as glorious Lord and Judge of all (1 Thess. 4:13–18; Matt. 25:31–32). He is now giving the Holy Spirit from the Father to all those who are truly his. The three Persons of the Trinity thus combine in the work of saving sinners.

This Gospel sets forth Jesus Christ as the living Savior, Master, Life, and Hope of all who put their trust in him. It tells us that the eternal destiny of all people depends on whether they are savingly related to Jesus Christ.

This Gospel is the only Gospel: there is no other; and to change its substance is to pervert and indeed destroy it. This Gospel is so simple that small children can understand it, and it is so profound that studies by the wisest theologians will never exhaust its riches.

All Christians are called to unity in love and unity in truth. As evangelicals who derive our very name from the Gospel, we celebrate this great good news of God's saving work in Jesus Christ as the true bond of Christian unity, whether among organized churches and denominations or in the many transdenominational cooperative enterprises of Christians together.

The Bible declares that all who truly trust in Christ and his Gospel are sons and daughters of God through grace, and hence are our brothers and sisters in Christ.

All who are justified experience reconciliation with the Father, full remission of sins, transition from the kingdom of darkness to the kingdom of light, the reality of being a new creature in Christ, and the fellowship of the Holy Spirit. They enjoy access to the Father with all the peace and joy that this brings.

The Gospel requires of all believers worship, which means constant praise and giving of thanks to God, submission to all that he has revealed in his written word, prayerful dependence on him, and vigilance lest his truth be even inadvertently compromised or obscured.

To share the joy and hope of this Gospel is a supreme privilege. It is also an abiding obligation, for the Great Commission of Jesus Christ still stands: proclaim the Gospel everywhere, he said, teaching, baptizing, and making disciples.

By embracing the following declaration we affirm our commitment to this task, and with it our allegiance to Christ himself, to the Gospel itself, and to each other as fellow evangelical believers.

The Gospel

This Gospel of Jesus Christ which God sets forth in the infallible Scriptures combines Jesus' own declaration of the present reality of the kingdom of God with the apostles' account of the person, place, and work of Christ, and how sinful humans benefit from it. The Patristic Rule of Faith, the historic creeds, the Reformation confessions, and the doctrinal bases of later evangelical bodies all witness to the substance of this biblical message.

The heart of the Gospel is that our holy, loving Creator, confronted with human hostility and rebellion, has chosen in his own freedom and faithfulness to become our holy, loving Redeemer and Restorer. The Father has sent the Son to be the Savior of the world (1 John 4:14): it is through his one and only Son that God's one and only plan of salvation is implemented. So Peter announced: "Salvation is found in no one else, for there is no other name under heaven given to men by which we must be saved" (Acts 4:12). And Christ himself taught: "I am the way, the truth and the life. No one comes to the Father except through me" (John 14:6).

Through the Gospel we learn that we human beings, who were made for fellowship with God, are by nature—that is, "in Adam" (1 Cor. 15:22)—dead in sin, unresponsive to and separated from our Maker. We are constantly twisting his truth, breaking his law, belittling his goals and standards, and offending his holiness by our unholiness, so that we truly are "without hope and without God in the world" (Rom. 1:18–32, 3:9–20; Eph. 2:1–3, 12). Yet God in grace took the initiative to reconcile us to himself through the sinless life and vicarious death of his beloved Son (Eph. 2:4–10; Rom. 3:21–24).

The Father sent the Son to free us from the dominion of sin and Satan, and to make us God's children and friends. Jesus paid our penalty in our place on his cross, satisfying the retributive demands of divine justice by shedding his blood in sacrifice and so making possible justification for all who trust in him (Rom. 3:25–26). The Bible describes this mighty substitutionary transaction as the achieving of ransom, reconciliation, redemption, propitiation, and conquest of evil powers (Matt. 20:28; 2 Cor. 5:18–21; Rom. 3:23–25; John 12:31; Col. 2:15). It secures for us a restored relationship with God that brings pardon and peace, acceptance and access, and adoption into God's family (Col. 1:20, 2:13–14; Rom. 5:1–2; Gal. 4:4–7; 1 Pet. 3:18). The faith in God and in Christ to which the Gospel calls us is a trustful outgoing of our hearts to lay hold of these promised and proffered benefits.

This Gospel further proclaims the bodily resurrection, ascension, and enthronement of Jesus as evidence of the efficacy of his once-for-all sacrifice for us, of the reality of his present personal ministry to us, and of the certainty of his future return to glorify us (1 Cor. 15; Heb. 1:1–4, 2:1–18, 4:14–16, 7:1–10:25). In the life of faith as the Gospel presents it, believers are united with their risen Lord, communing with him, and looking to him in repentance and hope for empowering through the Holy Spirit, so that henceforth they may not sin but serve him truly.

God's justification of those who trust him, according to the Gospel, is a decisive transition, here and now, from a state of condemnation and wrath because of their sins to one of acceptance and favor by virtue of Jesus' flawless obedience culminating in his voluntary sin-bearing death. God "justifies the wicked" (ungodly: Rom. 4:5) by imputing (reckoning, crediting, counting, accounting) righteousness to them and ceasing to count their sins against them (Rom. 4:1–8). Sinners receive through faith in Christ alone "the gift of righteousness" (Rom. 1:17, 5:17; Phil. 3:9) and thus become "the righteousness of God" in him who was "made sin" for them (2 Cor. 5:21).

As our sins were reckoned to Christ, so Christ's righteousness is reckoned to us. This is justification by the imputation of Christ's righteousness. All we bring to the transaction is our need of it. Our faith in the God who bestows it, the Father, the Son, and the Holy Spirit, is itself the fruit of God's grace. Faith links us savingly to Jesus, but inasmuch as it involves an acknowledgment that we have no merit of our own, it is confessedly not a meritorious work.

The Gospel assures us that all who have entrusted their lives to Jesus Christ are born-again children of God (John 1:12), indwelt, empowered, and assured of their status and hope by the Holy Spirit (Rom. 7:6, 8:9–17). The moment we truly believe in Christ, the Father declares us righteous in him and begins conforming us to his likeness. Genuine faith acknowledges and depends upon Jesus as Lord and shows itself in growing obedience to the divine commands, though this contributes nothing to the ground of our justification (James 2:14–26; Heb. 6:1–12).

By his sanctifying grace, Christ works within us through faith, renewing our fallen nature and leading us to real maturity, that measure of development which is meant by "the fullness of Christ" (Eph. 4:13). The Gospel calls us to live as obedient servants of Christ and as his emissaries in the world, doing justice, loving mercy, and helping all in need, thus seeking to bear witness to the kingdom of Christ. At death, Christ takes the believer to himself (Phil. 1:21) for unimaginable joy in the ceaseless worship of God (Rev. 22:1–5).

Salvation in its full sense is from the guilt of sin in the past, the power of sin in the present, and the presence of sin in the future. Thus, while in foretaste believers enjoy salvation now, they still await its fullness (Mark 14:61–62; Heb. 9:28). Salvation is a Trinitarian reality, initiated by the Father, implemented by the Son, and applied by the Holy Spirit. It has a global dimension, for God's plan is to save believers out of every tribe and tongue (Rev. 5:9) to be his church, a new humanity, the people of God, the body and bride of Christ, and the community of the Holy Spirit. All the heirs of final salvation are called here and now to serve their Lord and each other in love, to share in the fellowship of Jesus' sufferings, and to work together to make Christ known to the whole world.

We learn from the Gospel that, as all have sinned, so all who do not receive Christ will be judged according to their just deserts as measured by God's holy law, and face eternal retributive punishment.

Unity in the Gospel

Christians are commanded to love each other despite differences of race, gender, privilege, and social, political, and economic background (John 13:34–35; Gal. 3:28–29), and to be of one mind wherever possible (John 17:20–21; Phil. 2:2; Rom. 14:1–15:13). We know that divisions among Christians hinder our witness in the world, and we desire greater mutual understanding and truth-speaking in love. We know too that as trustees of God's revealed truth we cannot embrace any form of doctrinal indifferentism, or relativism, or pluralism by which God's truth is sacrificed for a false peace.

Doctrinal disagreements call for debate. Dialogue for mutual understanding and, if possible, narrowing of the differences is valuable, doubly so when the avowed goal is unity in primary things, with liberty in secondary things, and charity in all things.

In the foregoing paragraphs, an attempt has been made to state what is primary and essential in the Gospel as evangelicals understand it. Useful dialogue, however, requires not only charity in our attitudes, but also clarity in our utterances. Our extended analysis of justification by faith alone through Christ alone reflects our belief that Gospel truth is of crucial importance and is not always well understood and correctly affirmed. For added clarity, out of love for God's truth and Christ's church, we now cast the key points of what has been said into specific affirmations and denials regarding the Gospel and our unity in it and in Christ.

Affirmations and Denials

1. We affirm that the Gospel entrusted to the church is, in the first instance, God's Gospel (Mark 1:14; Rom. 1:1). God is its author, and he reveals it to us in and by his Word. Its authority and truth rest on him alone. □ We deny that the truth or authority of the Gospel derives from any human insight or invention (Gal. 1:1–11). We also deny that the truth or authority of the Gospel rests on the authority of any particular church or human institution.
2. We affirm that the Gospel is the saving power of God in that the Gospel effects salvation to everyone who believes, without distinction (Rom. 1:16). This efficacy of the Gospel is by the power of God himself (1 Cor. 1:18). □ We deny that the power of the Gospel rests in the eloquence of the preacher, the technique of the evangelist, or the persuasion of rational argument (1 Cor. 1:21; 2:1–5).
3. We affirm that the Gospel diagnoses the universal human condition as one of sinful rebellion against God, which, if unchanged, will lead each person to eternal loss under God's condemnation.

☐ We deny any rejection of the fallenness of human nature or any assertion of the natural goodness, or divinity, of the human race.

4. We affirm that Jesus Christ is the only way of salvation, the only mediator between God and humanity (John 14:6; 1 Tim. 2:5). ☐ We deny that anyone is saved in any other way than by Jesus Christ and his Gospel. The Bible offers no hope that sincere worshipers of other religions will be saved without personal faith in Jesus Christ.
5. We affirm that the church is commanded by God and is therefore under divine obligation to preach the Gospel to every living person (Luke 24:47; Matt. 28:18–19). ☐ We deny that any particular class or group of persons, whatever their ethnic or cultural identity, may be ignored or passed over in the preaching of the Gospel (1 Cor. 9:19–22). God purposes a global church made up from people of every tribe, language, and nation (Rev. 7:9).
6. We affirm that faith in Jesus Christ as the divine Word (or Logos, John 1:1), the second Person of the Trinity, co-eternal and co-essential with the Father and the Holy Spirit (Heb. 1:3), is foundational to faith in the Gospel. ☐ We deny that any view of Jesus Christ which reduces or rejects his full deity is Gospel faith or will avail to salvation.
7. We affirm that Jesus Christ is God incarnate (John 1:14). The virgin-born descendant of David (Rom. 1:3), he had a true human nature, was subject to the Law of God (Gal. 4:5), and was like us at all points, except without sin (Heb. 2:17, 7:26–28). We affirm that faith in the true humanity of Christ is essential to faith in the Gospel. ☐ We deny that anyone who rejects the humanity of Christ, his incarnation, or his sinlessness, or who maintains that these truths are not essential to the Gospel, will be saved (1 John 4:2–3).
8. We affirm that the atonement of Christ by which, in his obedience, he offered a perfect sacrifice, propitiating the Father by paying for our sins and satisfying divine justice on our behalf according to God's eternal plan, is an essential element of the Gospel. ☐ We deny that any view of the Atonement that rejects the substitutionary satisfaction of divine justice, accomplished vicariously for believers, is compatible with the teaching of the Gospel.
9. We affirm that Christ's saving work included both his life and his death on our behalf (Gal. 3:13). We declare that faith in the perfect obedience of Christ by which he fulfilled all the demands of the Law of God in our behalf is essential to the Gospel. ☐ We deny

that our salvation was achieved merely or exclusively by the death of Christ without reference to his life of perfect righteousness.

10. We affirm that the bodily resurrection of Christ from the dead is essential to the biblical Gospel (1 Cor. 15:14). □ We deny the validity of any so-called gospel that denies the historical reality of the bodily resurrection of Christ.
11. We affirm that the biblical doctrine of justification by faith alone in Christ alone is essential to the Gospel (Rom. 3:28; 4:5; Gal. 2:16). □ We deny that any person can believe the biblical Gospel and at the same time reject the apostolic teaching of justification by faith alone in Christ alone. We also deny that there is more than one true Gospel (Gal. 1:6–9).
12. We affirm that the doctrine of the imputation (reckoning or counting) both of our sins to Christ and of his righteousness to us, whereby our sins are fully forgiven and we are fully accepted, is essential to the biblical Gospel (2 Cor. 5:19–21). □ We deny that we are justified by the righteousness of Christ infused into us or by any righteousness that is thought to inhere within us.
13. We affirm that the righteousness of Christ by which we are justified is properly his own, which he achieved apart from us, in and by his perfect obedience. This righteousness is counted, reckoned, or imputed to us by the forensic (that is, legal) declaration of God, as the sole ground of our justification. □ We deny that any works we perform at any stage of our existence add to the merit of Christ or earn for us any merit that contributes in any way to the ground of our justification (Gal. 2:16; Eph. 2:8–9; Titus 3:5).
14. We affirm that, while all believers are indwelt by the Holy Spirit and are in the process of being made holy and conformed to the image of Christ, those consequences of justification are not its ground. God declares us just, remits our sins, and adopts us as his children, by his grace alone, and through faith alone, because of Christ alone, while we are still sinners (Rom. 4:5). □ We deny that believers must be inherently righteous by virtue of their cooperation with God's life-transforming grace before God will declare them justified in Christ. We are justified while we are still sinners.
15. We affirm that saving faith results in sanctification, the transformation of life in growing conformity to Christ through the power of the Holy Spirit. Sanctification means ongoing repentance, a life of turning from sin to serve Jesus Christ in grateful reliance on him as one's Lord and Master (Gal. 5:22–25; Rom. 8:4, 13–14). □ We reject any view of justification which divorces it from our sancti-

fying union with Christ and our increasing conformity to his image through prayer, repentance, cross-bearing, and life in the Spirit.

16. We affirm that saving faith includes mental assent to the content of the Gospel, acknowledgment of our own sin and need, and personal trust and reliance upon Christ and his work. □ We deny that saving faith includes only mental acceptance of the Gospel, and that justification is secured by a mere outward profession of faith. We further deny that any element of saving faith is a meritorious work or earns salvation for us.
17. We affirm that, although true doctrine is vital for spiritual health and well-being, we are not saved by doctrine. Doctrine is necessary to inform us how we may be saved by Christ, but it is Christ who saves. □ We deny that the doctrines of the Gospel can be rejected without harm. Denial of the Gospel brings spiritual ruin and exposes us to God's judgment.
18. We affirm that Jesus Christ commands his followers to proclaim the Gospel to all living persons, evangelizing everyone everywhere, and discipling believers within the fellowship of the church. A full and faithful witness to Christ includes the witness of personal testimony, godly living, and acts of mercy and charity to our neighbor, without which the preaching of the Gospel appears barren. □ We deny that the witness of personal testimony, godly living, and acts of mercy and charity to our neighbors constitutes evangelism apart from the proclamation of the Gospel.

Our Commitment

As evangelicals united in the Gospel, we promise to watch over and care for one another, to pray for and forgive one another, and to reach out in love and truth to God's people everywhere, for we are one family, one in the Holy Spirit, and one in Christ.

Centuries ago it was truly said that in things necessary there must be unity, in things less than necessary there must be liberty, and in all things there must be charity. We see all these Gospel truths as necessary.

Now to God, the Author of the truth and grace of this Gospel, through Jesus Christ, its subject and our Lord, be praise and glory for ever and ever. Amen.

The Gospel of Jesus Christ: Part 1

1. We affirm that the gospel entrusted to the church is, in the first instance, God's gospel.
2. We affirm that the gospel is the saving power of God in that the gospel effects salvation to everyone who believes, without distinction.
3. We affirm that the gospel diagnoses the universal human condition as one of sinful rebellion against God.
4. We affirm that Jesus Christ is the only way of salvation.

7

The Saving Power of God

As we have read in *The Gospel of Jesus Christ,* "the key points" of the first part of this statement are, in the second part, "cast . . . into specific affirmations and denials regarding the Gospel." This chapter will explain the first four of these affirmations and denials, with remaining chapters explaining the rest of them. The first affirmation deals with the question of ownership: Does the gospel belong to human beings and institutions? Or does it belong to God himself?

God's Gospel

> 1. We affirm that the Gospel entrusted to the church is, in the first instance, God's Gospel (Mark 1:14; Rom. 1:1). God is its author, and he reveals it to us in and by his Word. Its authority and truth rest on him alone. ☐ We deny that the truth or authority of the Gospel derives from any human insight or invention (Gal. 1:1–11). We also deny that the truth or author-

ity of the Gospel rests on the authority of any particular church or human institution.

In the opening words of his Letter to the Romans, Paul speaks of himself as one called to declare "the gospel of God" (Rom. 1:1). The word *of* here indicates possession. That is, the gospel Paul is called to proclaim is not merely good news about God. Rather the gospel is God's possession. It is his property. In this regard the original owner and author of the gospel is God himself.

The gospel is good news that God *gives* to the church. It is a gracious gift, a gift that cannot be deserved. The means by which God gives the gospel to the church is Christ and his apostles. This does not negate the extent to which the gospel is already proclaimed in the Old Testament. That is, the affirmation that the gospel is given to the church refers to the historic New Testament church, which received the gospel chiefly by Christ and the apostles, but not exclusively by them because the Old Testament prepared the way for the New Testament declaration of the gospel.

When the Apostle Paul wrote his Epistle to the Romans, he began by declaring: "Paul, a servant of Jesus Christ, called to be an apostle, separated to the gospel of God which He promised before through His prophets in the Holy Scriptures, concerning His Son Jesus Christ our Lord, who was born of the seed of David according to the flesh, and declared to be the Son of God with power, according to the Spirit of holiness, by the resurrection from the dead" (Rom. 1:1–4).

Here Paul links the gospel of God with that which was promised through the Old Testament Scriptures. The New Testament frequently refers to the work of Christ as being "according to the Scriptures."

Though there are elements of newness in the New Covenant and therefore elements of discontinuity with the Old Covenant, the New Covenant is linked to and grows out of the Old Covenant. There remains a solid stratum of continuity between the two so that there is no radical disjunction between them. Jesus himself frequently called attention to this continuity by saying things like "Moses wrote of me" and "Abraham rejoiced to see my day." The earliest narratives of the gospel emphasize this link to the past. In the Magnificat Mary says: "He has helped His servant Israel, in remembrance of His mercy, as He spoke to our fathers, to Abraham and to his seed forever" (Luke 1:54–55).

In like manner Zacharias refers liberally to the Old Testament: "Blessed is the Lord God of Israel, for He has visited and redeemed His people, and has raised up a horn of salvation for us in the house of His servant David, as He spoke by the mouth of His holy prophets ... to perform the mercy promised to our fathers and to remember His holy covenant, the oath which He swore to our father Abraham. . . ." (Luke 1:68–70, 72).

The New Testament claims that Jesus appeared in the "fullness of time" and that the context in which he performed his saving work was the context of history.

This point has been sorely disputed in twentieth-century New Testament scholarship, particularly in light of the innovations wrought by Rudolf Bultmann. Bultmann sought a "theology of timelessness" in which salvation is understood strictly in vertical terms. Salvation is "punctiliar" in that it always occurs in an existential "moment of decision" in the "here and now" *(hic et nunc)*. For Bultmann and many of his followers, the question of Jesus' historicity is irrelevant. Salvation is ripped out of its historical context and assigned to some supratemporal plane. For this reason some of Bultmann's critics called him a neo-Gnostic. Skepticism regarding the real historical Jesus has threatened the reality of the gospel as it is ripped from its moorings in real history.

Some have argued that in the biblical record we are dealing with, not ordinary history, but "redemptive history," with the accent on "redemptive." Others, such as Oscar Cullmann and Herman N. Ridderbos, while agreeing that the Bible is redemptive history, insist that it remains redemptive *history*. To negate that historical reality is to repudiate the redemption proclaimed in the gospel. A gospel that is nonhistorical or suprahistorical is no gospel at all.

The beginnings of the revelation of the gospel are found early in the Book of Genesis in the so-called "proto-evangel" or "first gospel." Ironically the context for the first gospel is not "good news" but bad news, not benediction but malediction. The immediate context of the proto-evangel is God's curse on the beguiling serpent in the garden: ". . . the LORD God said to the serpent: 'Because you have done this, you are cursed more than all cattle, and more than every beast of the field; on your belly you shall go, and you shall eat dust all the days of your life. And I will put enmity between you and the woman, and between your seed and her Seed; He shall bruise your head, and you shall bruise His heel.'" (Gen. 3:14–15)

This is certainly bad news for the serpent. Yet malediction to Satan is benediction for us. The cryptic prophetic content of the curse speaks of the serpent's seed having his head crushed under the foot of the woman's Seed, but not without the serpent's seed inflicting injury to the heel of the woman's Seed. Fortunately for us and our salvation, the heel of the woman's Seed is not the heel of Achilles.

The church has seen in this proto-evangel a veiled reference to the cross on which Christ is bruised while conquering the works of the devil. It is clear how Old Testament prophecies regarding the promised Messiah and his redemptive work bear witness to the gospel. What is often overlooked is the relationship between the Old Testament law and the gospel. Though we distinguish between law and gospel, it would be the greatest folly to separate them. We remember that the law of God is also the Word of God and that the Word of God is law.

Paul articulates the link between law and gospel when he writes:

> What purpose then does the law serve? It was added because of transgressions, till the Seed should come to whom the promise was made; and it was appointed through angels by the hand of a mediator. Now a mediator does not mediate for one only, but God is one. Is the law then against the promises of God? Certainly not! For if there had been a law given which could have given life, truly righteousness would have been by the law. But the Scripture has confined all under sin, that the promise by faith in Jesus Christ might be given to those who believe. But before faith came, we were kept under guard by the law, kept for the faith which would afterward be revealed. Therefore the law was our tutor to bring us to Christ, that we might be justified by faith. (Gal. 3:19–24)

Far from repudiating the gospel, the law indirectly bears witness to the gospel. The law is expressed in terms of blessings and curses, curses taken by Christ upon himself and blessings won for us by his perfect obedience. The promised blessings of the law are fulfilled in the gospel, while the law serves as our schoolmaster to bring us to Christ. The law reveals God as one who heaps blessing on perfect righteousness and pours out wrath on all wickedness.

That the Old Testament proclaims the gospel is seen vividly in the New Testament account of Jesus' postresurrection appearance to the men on the road to Emmaus. While conversing with them, Jesus rebuked them: "'O foolish ones, and slow of heart to believe in all that the prophets have spoken! Ought not the Christ to have suffered these things and to enter into His glory?' And beginning at Moses and all the Prophets, He expounded to them in all the Scriptures the things concerning Himself." (Luke 24:25–27)

Two important principles underlie the first affirmation in *The Gospel of Jesus Christ.* First, Christianity is a revealed religion. Its content is not the result of speculative human philosophy, nor of a fortuitous evolutionary process of human insight or custom. The source of its content and truth is God himself. Central to that content is the truth of the gospel.

Second, Scripture, as the Word of God, is also revelatory, and its authority rests on the authority of its ultimate source. Implied in this first affirmation is the evangelical principle of *sola Scriptura,* at least to the extent that the authority of the gospel resides in the Word of God precisely because it is the Word of *God.*

In the New Testament, elements of the gospel are proclaimed by angels, John the Baptist, and others, but chiefly by Christ himself and his appointed apostles. An apostle is one who speaks with the authority of the one who has sent him. In this regard the chief apostle in the New Testament is Christ himself, who is sent by the Father and speaks by virtue of his Father's delegated authority. He reveals to us what was given to him by the Father to reveal. Indeed he reveals the Father himself. Jesus is the zenith of God's special revelation, so that in his teaching and in himself we find the very essence of the gospel.

In turn, Jesus delegated authority to his early apostles, who declared his word with his authority. The apostles, like prophets in the Old Testament, were agents of divine revelation. The authority goes from the Father to the Son and from the Son to the apostles.

The gospel comes to us by divine tradition. Here we must distinguish sharply between the divine tradition and human traditions. Jesus rebuked the Pharisees for replacing the divine tradition with their own humanly contrived traditions. But this does not deny that there is a divine tradition found in Scripture. We commonly refer to it as the apostolic tradition, passed on to us via the Scriptures. Again we note that the apostolic tradition was what the apostles themselves first received from Christ.

The gospel is integral to the apostolic and divine tradition. The gospel is not derived from mere human tradition. We see a link between the words *author* and *authority.* Because God is the original author of the gospel, the gospel carries the weight of his authority. This authority carries the intrinsic right to command obedience, impose obligation, and bind the human conscience. No human authority carries such weight *intrinsically.*

Just as the gospel's authority rests ultimately in God, so does its truth. Any message that originates with God, the fountain of all truth, carries the mark of his inherent truthfulness. It is impossible for God to lie. There is no falsehood or defect in anything he declares. In this respect, since the gospel comes to us by divine declaration, it comes to us as infallible truth. Again the infallibility of that truth rests on the infallibility of God himself.

It is of the greatest comfort and consolation to the Christian to be assured that the gospel is God's gospel. Since it is his gospel, its promises cannot fail.

Article 1 denies that the truth or authority of the gospel rests on the authority of any particular church or human institution.

Here we see a parallel between the Scripture in general and the gospel in particular. In the Reformation principle of *sola Scriptura,* the Reformers insisted that the church gains whatever authority she possesses from the Bible. The Bible does not, as Rome declared, gain its authority from the church. The ancient church had understood that the church "receives" the Bible and submits to it. The church does not create Scripture or give to it its authority. In like manner the authority of the gospel is not dependent on the authority of the church. The church does not create the gospel. The church receives the gospel and has the sacred duty to proclaim the gospel in its purity.

God's Power

2. We affirm that the Gospel is the saving power of God in that the Gospel effects salvation to everyone who believes, without distinction (Rom. 1:16). This efficacy of the Gospel is by the power of God himself (1 Cor. 1:18). ☐ We deny that the power of the Gospel rests in the eloquence of the preacher, the technique of the evangelist, or the persuasion of rational argument (1 Cor. 1:21; 2:1–5).

In his Letter to the Romans the Apostle Paul says, ". . . I am not ashamed of the gospel of Christ, for it is the power of God to salvation for everyone who believes. . . ." (Rom. 1:16). In these words Paul assigns power to the gospel. He reinforces this idea in 1 Corinthians: ". . . the message of the cross is foolishness to those who are perishing, but to us who are being saved it is the power of God" (1 Cor. 1:18). As the Word of God the gospel is more powerful than a two-edged sword, able to cut to the core of the human heart.

The power of the gospel is not found simply in the words that express it. The message is powerful because the word is accompanied by the working of the Holy Spirit, who himself is the power of God. It is as if the gospel were a weapon in the hands of God, gaining its efficacy from the power of God himself.

The Scriptures teach that God has chosen the foolishness of preaching as the means by which he effects salvation for the believer. This power is given only to those who believe, yet the source of the gospel's power is not the faith of the believer. It is not the power of the believer that makes the gospel effective unto salvation. That power resides in God, who by his Holy Spirit applies the effects of the gospel to those who believe. Salvation is always of the Lord, and it is accomplished by and through his power.

If we are careful to distinguish between the gospel and the Spirit's power, we must be equally careful not to separate them. The Holy Spirit works in and by the preaching of the gospel. Without the power of the Holy Spirit our preaching would be in vain, but with the Spirit's power our preaching is never in vain. Again, our comfort and confidence in the enterprise of evangelism rest on God's promise that his Word does not return to him empty or void. The preaching of the gospel is not an exercise in impotency.

Article 2 denies that the gospel's power rests in the preacher's eloquence, the evangelist's technique, or the apologist's argument.

This denial is not meant to denigrate homiletical skill or eloquence. That preachers hone their verbal skills and sermonic delivery is not a bad thing. These aspects of human skill, however, are not sufficient to effect salvation. They are no substitute for the power of God. The Apostle Paul wrote to the Corinthians: "... when I came to you, [I] did not come with excellence of speech or of wisdom declaring to you the testimony of God. For I determined not to know anything among you except Jesus Christ and Him crucified. I was with you in weakness, in fear, and in much trembling. And my speech and my preaching were not with persuasive words of human wisdom, but in demonstration of the Spirit and of power, that your faith should not be in the wisdom of men but in the power of God." (1 Cor. 2:1–5)

Paul is not indulging in false modesty. He was not an inept speaker, nor was he inarticulate. A cursory reading of his epistle demonstrates that Paul was a learned man and a skilled communicator. He was supremely articulate and a master of verbal expression. Yet he understood clearly that whatever efficacy he had as a preacher was due in the final analysis, not to his own talent, but to the power of the Holy Spirit as it accompanied the preaching of the pure gospel.

It is the purity of the gospel that should be the evangelist's chief concern. Accuracy in setting forth the biblical message is supremely more important than human devices like oratorical eloquence. Eloquence without the Spirit is impotent.

To stress such a fundamental point about preaching may be like carrying coals to Newcastle. It seems elementary to point out such an obvious truism. It is a truth, however, that is as easy to forget as it is to grasp initially. The modern preacher who speaks to people accustomed to high-tech forms of communication—replete with the bells and whistles of entertainment and carefully orchestrated media enhancements—is under constant and enormous pressure to embellish his message with entertainment, lest he commit the cardinal sin of communication and bore his audience. But the gospel, clearly and accurately set forth, is never boring when energized by the power of God. No message is more gripping. When the gospel is declared purely and boldly, it unleashes the power of God.

Evangelism in our time has become an art form. Techniques and methods have been studied, analyzed, and perfected as marketing skills. Statistics show that certain response levels can be predicted as the formulas are implemented. What cannot be predicted or controlled by such techniques is the sovereign operation of God's Spirit. A certain technique may guarantee a predictable number of professions of faith, but such professions may or may not be genuine. No evangelistic technique can guarantee the operation of the Holy Spirit on the hearer's heart. We can move people to raise their hands, pray a prayer, walk the aisle, or declare a decision, but we cannot move a person to saving faith. That is not within our power. Only the Spirit of God can effect that change.

The New Testament calls us to give reasons for the faith we declare. Preaching the gospel is not a license for sloppy thinking or irrational assertions. Our preaching should be done with a sound mind and sound thinking. Paul argued daily in the marketplace, reasoning carefully with his hearers. He presented rational arguments that were solid. But obviously the apostle understood the difference between proof and persuasion. God himself in nature, history, and his Word has given incontrovertible proof of his own existence and the true identity of Christ. Yet multitudes who hear and see such proof remain unpersuaded because sin has so clouded their minds and captured their hearts. "... no one knows the things of God except the Spirit of God," Paul writes. "Now we have received, not the spirit of the world, but the Spirit who is from God, that we might know the things that have been freely given to us by God." (1 Cor. 2:11–12)

Rebellion against God

> 3. We affirm that the Gospel diagnoses the universal human condition as one of sinful rebellion against God, which, if unchanged, will lead each person to eternal loss under God's condemnation. ☐ We deny any rejection of the fallenness of human nature or any assertion of the natural goodness, or divinity, of the human race.

Though the content of the gospel does not include the notion of sin, it does presuppose the idea of human fallenness. That is, the good news of the gospel includes a message of reconciliation, which necessarily presupposes a prior estrangement requiring reconciliation. The good news is that there is a remedy for our sins and our rebellion against God.

In this sense the gospel is, among other things, *diagnostic.* It both diagnoses the problem and prescribes a cure. The announcement of redemption and salvation comes as the antidote to eternal condemnation.

In including an affirmation and denial regarding the universal human condition of sinful rebellion, the framers of *The Gospel of Jesus Christ* follow the lead of the Apostle Paul in his exposition of the gospel in the Epistle to the Romans. After declaring the theme of "the righteousness of God [that] is revealed from faith to faith" (Rom. 1:17), Paul moves quickly to the revelation of God's wrath directed against all ungodliness and unrighteousness of men. Paul explains that men universally repress God's revelation of himself in nature, and that although they knew God they did not glorify him as God, nor were they thankful.

From this basic rejection of God's self-revelation, Paul moves to the radical corruption that flows from it, showing that both Jew and Gentile are under divine judgment. All people must stand before the tribunal of God, and under the law all are declared guilty.

"We know," Paul writes, "that whatever the law says, it says to those who are under the law, that every mouth may be stopped, and all the world may become guilty before God. Therefore by the deeds of the law no flesh will be justified in His sight, for by the law is the knowledge of sin." (Rom. 3:19–20)

Before explaining the gospel, Paul reminds us of our status under the law: We are judged guilty. The law is powerless to save in that all have sinned and fallen short of God's glory.

The good news of the gospel is announced to those who have been so judged. This is the dilemma presupposed by the gospel: God is just and we are unjust. We are in desperate need of the justification the gospel proclaims.

Article 3 denies all rejections of original sin, our fallen corrupt condition. The humanist credo, which declares the basic goodness of humanity, is denied. Those who see sin as merely tangential, peripheral, or accidental, and not systemic in the core of our fallen humanity, are in view here.

The denial's final clause is aimed at the neo-Gnostic view that human beings are little gods. The New Age philosophy that pervades American culture and has penetrated the evangelical church is here denied. This article allows no room for the apotheosis of human beings. The promise of the deification of humans has its origin in the Garden of Eden with the serpent's lie, "You will be like God" (Gen. 3:5).

The Only Way

> 4. We affirm that Jesus Christ is the only way of salvation, the only mediator between God and humanity (John 14:6; 1 Tim. 2:5). ☐ We deny that anyone is saved in any other way than by Jesus Christ and his Gospel. The Bible offers no hope that sincere worshipers of other religions will be saved without personal faith in Jesus Christ.

The Bible offers people no hope apart from personal faith in Christ. The Bible teaches that he is unique. Perhaps no tenet of Christianity is more repugnant to the postmodern world than this claim of exclusivity. The field of comparative religion and the prevailing spirit of pluralism and relativism recoil at such an exclusive claim for Christ. The culture perceives such a claim as intolerant bigotry, arrogance, or religious triumphalism; as demeaning to adherents of other religions—Jews, Muslims, Buddhists, and others.

Yet the Scriptures claim unambiguously that Jesus is the "only begotten" of the Father (John 3:16). If the claim to Christ's uniqueness and exclusivity rested merely on the declaration of the church or the individual Christian, it could and probably would warrant the charge of arrogant bigotry. If Christians believed Christ is the only way to salvation simply because he is their way, the charge would be valid. Yet the church's confession does not rest on the premise that "my way must be the only way, because it is my way."

At this point the church is submitting to and echoing the claims of Jesus himself. In John's Gospel Jesus declares: "I am the way, the truth, and the life. No one comes to the Father except through Me." (John 14:6) Here is exclusivity with a vengeance. Jesus uses a universal negative proposition when he says "no one comes to the Father except through Me." The term *except* indicates a condition that must be met for a result to occur. The result in view is coming to the Father. The necessary condition is that it must occur "through Me."

Jesus is the "door" people must enter to gain access to God. In emphatic terms Jesus asserted: "Most assuredly, I say to you, I am the door of the sheep. All who ever came before Me are thieves and robbers, but the sheep did not hear them. I am the door. If anyone enters by Me, he will be saved, and will go in and out and find pasture." (John 10:7–9)

As Paul declared, "... there is one God and one Mediator between God and men, the Man Christ Jesus. . . ." (1 Tim. 2:5). Jesus is the only way of salvation because he alone is the Mediator between God and men. That Christ is our Mediator is part of the gospel. In a lesser sense others have served in the role of mediator between God and his people. Anyone who acts as a "go-between" between God and man can be referred to as mediator. In the Old Testament Moses stood between God and the people, serving as an arbiter, an intercessor, and an advocate. Insofar as prophets mediated the Word of God to the people, they too were "mediators." Likewise the priests who spoke to God in behalf of the people and offered sacrifices were involved in mediation. Even angels, as messengers of God, functioned as intermediate agents of revelation.

In light of these multiple instances of mediation, why did Paul declare there is only one Mediator between God and man? Perhaps the answer is found in Paul's use of the present tense. In the past there were several mediators, but at present in redemptive history there remains only one, Jesus.

Though this is a possible interpretation of Paul's declaration, it is neither a necessary nor even a likely one. In all probability Paul has in view the overall uniqueness of Christ as our mediator. He is not only *a* mediator; he is *the* Mediator. He is the Mediator par excellence and in a special sense our Mediator *sui generis*. He alone is the God-man. He alone is the only begotten of the Father. By virtue of Christ's dual nature—*vere homo* ("truly man") and *vere Deus* ("truly God")—he is utterly unique.

In the ancient Greek world a "mediator" *(mesitēs)* stood in the middle of estranged parties and intervened to effect reconciliation. This is the language of the New Testament concept of salvation. By sin we are estranged from and at enmity with God. Christ performs the work of reconciliation at the Father's behest: ". . . all things are of God, who has reconciled us to Himself through Jesus Christ, and has given us the ministry of reconciliation, that is, that God was in Christ reconciling the world to Himself, not imputing their trespasses to them, and has committed to us the word of reconciliation" (2 Cor. 5:18–19).

In his office as mediator Christ reconciles us with God. This could not be accomplished by any other. The supremacy of Christ as mediator is labored by the author of Hebrews, who shows Christ's superiority to the angels: ". . . to which of the angels did He ever say: 'You are My Son, today I have begotten You'? And again: 'I will be to Him a Father, and He shall be to Me a Son'? But when He again brings the firstborn into the world, He says: 'Let all the angels of God worship Him.'" (Heb. 1:5–6) Later the author of Hebrews adds: "But to which of the angels has He ever said: 'Sit at My right hand, till I make Your enemies Your footstool'?" (Heb. 1:13).

In similar fashion the author of Hebrews shows Christ's superiority to Moses: ". . . consider the Apostle and High Priest of our confession, Christ Jesus, who was faithful to Him who appointed Him, as Moses also was faithful in all His house. For this One has been counted worthy of more glory than Moses, inasmuch as He who built the house has more honor than the house. For every house is built by someone, but He who built all things is God. And Moses indeed was faithful in all His house as a servant, for a testimony of those things which would be spoken afterward, but Christ as a Son over His own house, whose house we are. . . ." (Heb. 3:1–6)

John Calvin developed the concept of Christ's three-fold office *(munus triplex)* as Prophet, Priest, and King. Jesus was not merely *a* prophet, he was also *the* Prophet. He was both the subject and object of prophecy. That is, he was both a prophet himself and the chief object of biblical prophecy. The fulfillment of prophecies converges in his person and work. Thus Jesus was superior to Old Testament prophets.

Likewise, Jesus was superior to Old Testament priests. He was not only *a* priest, but also *the* Priest. He was both subject and object of priesthood. Like the priests he offered an atoning sacrifice. Unlike them the sacrifice he offered was himself. His offering was once-for-all. It was the full reality that the offerings of the Old Testament had merely foreshadowed.

Hebrews also asserts that Christ's priesthood is superior to the Levitical priesthood, showing that Christ's priesthood is after the order of Melchizedek and that Christ's priesthood endures forever. Hebrews says of Christ: ". . . such a High Priest was fitting for us, who is holy, harmless, undefiled, separate from sinners, and has become higher than the heavens; who does not need daily, as those high priests, to offer up sacrifices, first for His own sins and then for the people's, for this He did once for all when He offered up Himself. For the law appoints as high priests men who have weakness, but the word of the oath, which came after the law, appoints the Son who has been perfected forever." (Heb. 7:26–28)

In the Old Testament the king was anointed by God to serve as God's vice-regent. The king possessed no autonomous authority, but was subject to the King's law. When anointing Saul as Israel's first king, Samuel gave a solemn warning: ". . . here is the king whom you have chosen and whom you have desired. And take note, the LORD has set a king over you. If you fear the LORD and serve Him and obey His voice, and do not rebel against the commandment of the LORD, then both you and the king who reigns over you will continue following the LORD your God. However, if you do not obey the voice of the LORD, but rebel against the commandment of the LORD, then the hand of the LORD will be against you, as it was against your fathers." (1 Sam. 12:13–15)

The rest of the Old Testament is a testimony to the disobedience of both the people and their kings. The list of kings, especially in the northern kingdom, reads like a rogues' gallery. The one bright spot was the kingship of David, who despite his shortcomings was beloved of God. Yet David wrote about a greater Son who would also be David's Lord.

The kings of the Old Testament were supposed to function as mediators, but in the main they performed miserably. In Christ, to whom the kingdom of God is given, we meet one who is not only *a* king, but *the* King. He is designated the King of kings, the superlative expression of royalty. To him is given all authority in heaven and on earth. He sits on the right hand of God, where he exercises cosmic dominion. He is the supreme King who at the same time is our great High Priest and our primary Advocate with the Father.

In all these ways and more, we see Christ as our unique Mediator, who through his person and work effects our salvation. No other creature is worthy to be compared to him, who is the only way to the Father.

Article 4 denies that we are saved any other way than through Jesus Christ and his gospel. This follows from the uniqueness of his person and the sole sufficiency of his work. No one else qualifies to reconcile God and man, estranged by sin. No other religious leader was a God-man. No other religious leader has atoned for the sins of his people. Christ and Christ alone was sinless and qualified to offer the perfect sacrifice to satisfy the demands of God's justice. There is no other name under heaven through which men must be saved (Acts 4:12).

Religion that rejects Christ, no matter how sincere, is under divine judgment. Religion that is not in harmony with the truth of God is, as Paul clearly articulates, exposed to the wrath of God (Rom. 1:18–19). False religions are examples of idolatry, the most basic and common human sin. When Paul encountered the philosophers at Mar's Hill in Athens, he declared: "Truly, these times of ignorance God overlooked, but now commands all men everywhere to repent, because He has appointed a day on which He will judge the world in righteousness by the Man whom He has ordained. He has given assurance of this to all by raising Him from the dead." (Acts 17:30–31)

Paul boldly declares that the gospel is no mere offer that can be rejected with impunity, but a divine command that imposes obligation. God commands us to preach the gospel to every creature because he commands every creature to embrace it. There is no uncertainty about the identity of "the Man," because Paul says this Man has been raised from the dead. The resurrection was God's vindication of his only-begotten, our Mediator, who alone could make atonement for sin and reconcile us to God.

Muhammad made no atonement and Muhammad is dead. Buddha made no atonement and Buddha is dead. Confucius made no atonement and Confucius is dead. These religious leaders were capable of saving no one, not even themselves. Faith in them or in their teaching is not adequate for salvation. Until the church understands this, believes it, and acts on it, the church will not proclaim the gospel to all people and the church will be disobeying the Great Commission (Matt. 28:19).

The Gospel of Jesus Christ: Part 2

5. We affirm that the church is commanded by God to preach the gospel to every living person.
6. We affirm that faith in Jesus Christ as the divine Word is foundational to faith in the gospel.
7. We affirm that faith in the true humanity of Christ is essential to faith in the gospel.

Christ the Incarnation of God

What is Christ's Great Commission to his church? Article 5 of *The Gospel of Jesus Christ* restates this commission.

The Church's Duty

> 5. We affirm that the church is commanded by God and is therefore under divine obligation to preach the Gospel to every living person (Luke 24:47; Matt. 28:18–19). □ We deny that any particular class or group of persons, whatever their ethnic or cultural identity, may be ignored or passed over in the preaching of the Gospel (1 Cor. 9:19–22). God purposes a global church made up from people of every tribe, language, and nation (Rev. 7:9).

Jesus commissioned the church to "go into all the world and preach the gospel to every creature" (Mark 16:15). The term *mission* comes from the Latin verb meaning "to send." Many

English words derive from this root, such as *missile, permission, missive,* and *commission.* The task of world missions was not invented by the Christian community or determined by an agenda of power politics. This task was assigned to the church by Christ himself. Christ did not found the church and leave it up to his followers to determine the church's agenda. As Lord of the church and Head of his body, he defined the church's mission: to preach the gospel to all people.

Many churches borrow a page from secular business by crafting a carefully worded "mission statement." This statement is intended to delimit the chief purpose of the organization and to guide corporate decisions. The strategies and tactics employed by the organization are evaluated in terms of their conformity to and support of its mission statement. The popular method of "management by objective," which involves setting particular goals and objectives, is done with a view toward accomplishing the purpose of the organization. An objective is one of the general things that will be done to achieve the purpose. Goals are more specific, being quantifiable means for reaching the objectives. The classic formula for a goal is this: to + an action verb + a quantifiable noun + a date.

For example, if my objective at home is to make my yard more beautiful (which in itself is difficult to measure), I may set a goal "to plant five flowering trees by May 30." On that day I will know clearly the extent to which my goal has been reached.

These modern methods may be of service to the church, but only if the church is first clear about its mission and purpose.

During the Reformation, with the proliferation of sects and denominations, Christians faced the question, What are the marks of a true church? For the Reformers the first defining mark of a true church is that it preaches the gospel. Any religious body that is not preaching the gospel they did not consider a true or valid church. Because the Reformers believed that *sola fide* is essential to the gospel, and because Rome rejected *sola fide,* the Reformers could no longer consider Rome a true or valid church. However orthodox Rome was at other points, she was missing the first and chief mark of a true church.

Paraministry organizations exist for the sole purpose of engaging in evangelism. Such organizations are involved in a noble cause and have a legitimate purpose, but they are not churches. Preaching the gospel is one mark of a true church, but it is not the only one. A church is not a church if it fails to preach the gospel, but preaching the gospel does not make an organization a church.

The task of evangelism is not the same as the task of Christian education. The two are closely related, but they may be distinguished from each other. Scholars have analyzed the content of apostolic preaching, particularly with respect to sermons recorded in the Book of Acts. This preaching is often called *kērygma,* a Greek word meaning "preaching" or "proclamation." *Kērygma* is distinguished from *didachē,* another Greek word meaning "teaching."

In the apostolic community *kērygma* was the proclamation of the gospel, a summary of the person and work of Christ and a call to receive him by faith. Those who responded affirmatively were welcomed into the church community, where they then received catechetical instruction in the wider content and doctrines of the faith, which was the *didachē.* The first step was *kērygma,* preaching the content of the gospel. Today we see churches engaged in evangelism with little or no doctrinal instruction. They have *kērygma,* but little or no *didachē.* We also see churches that are heavy on theological instruction but light on evangelism. These groups have *didachē* with little or no *kērygma.* If indeed there is no *kērygma,* then the gospel is not being proclaimed and the "church" is not a church.

The very term *church* is derived from a possessive form of the Greek word for "Lord," *Kyrios.* In this sense the church refers to those who belong to the Lord. To belong to him is to be under his authority and to obey his agenda.

Every church has a mission, because every church is a group of people who have been "sent." That sending is both a mission and a commission. We have been commissioned by Christ to preach the gospel.

In preaching the gospel the church bears witness to the kingdom of Christ. The last question the disciples asked Jesus before he departed from them was this: "Lord, will You at this time restore the kingdom to Israel?" (Acts 1:6). It is significant that the disciples' final query concerned the kingdom. Jesus' answer is crucial for the church to grasp: "It is not for you to know times or seasons which the Father has put in His own authority. But you shall receive power when the Holy Spirit has come upon you; and you shall be witnesses to Me in Jerusalem, and in all Judea and Samaria, and to the end of the earth." (Acts 1:7–8)

When Jesus said "you shall be witnesses," he was not simply predicting the apostles' future activity. This was no mere future prophecy. The word *shall* expresses an imperative, Christ's last command before departing from this world.

The scope of this command is also noteworthy. It includes a geographical and, by implication, an ethnic scope. The witnessing was to take place locally in Jerusalem, in the broader locale of Judea, then extending to Samaria, and finally reaching to the ends of the earth. This could be seen as the thematic statement for the whole Book of Acts. Luke traces the growth of the early church as it began in Jerusalem, spread to Judea and Samaria, and then through Paul's missionary outreach to the Gentile world.

We see in Acts that the scope of the church's mission was defined not merely in geographical terms, but also in ethnic terms. One of the most pressing questions faced by the pristine church was the status of groups that had failed to be fully included in the Old Testament community: "God-fearers" (Gentile converts to Judaism), Samaritans (with whom the Jews had no dealings), and Gentiles. Acts makes it clear that people from all these groups received the gospel and were given full membership status in the church. The early church was polyethnic, with a wide diversity of ethnic and socio-economic groups. It included Jew and Greek, slave and free, rich and poor. In a word, the gospel was being preached to all groups of people and was restricted to no particular group.

I once learned this ditty: "Ornithological species of the same or similar plumage tend to habitually congregate in the closest possible proximity." This expresses a more popular adage: "Birds of a feather flock together." This adage is borne out in the socio-economic and ethnic composition of many, if not most, contemporary churches. Polls indicate that our denominations tend to be homogenous. I am not sure why this happens, and I trust it is not by design. It seems to be human nature to congregate with people similar to ourselves. We tend to suffer from xenophobia, the fear of people different from ourselves.

We must be aware of these tendencies and seek to overcome them, lest we fall into the trap of targeting only affinity groups with the gospel. This is in view in article 5's denial. Though the church in America has aggressively supported the sending of missionaries into Muslim, Buddhist, and Shinto countries, it has been far less aggressive in preaching to adherents of other religions who reside in our own country. We tend to shy away from evangelizing Jews or Muslims in our midst.

There may be many reasons for our reticence. We all recognize that evangelistic outreach to people of other religions is dangerous business, because it is fiercely resisted by the leaders of these religions. If you doubt this, ask Moishe Rosen, head of Jews for Jesus. To proselytize adherents of other religions in America is the height of political incorrectness.

Our country was founded on a principle of religious toleration. All religions are regarded as being equal under the law. It is a short step from equal toleration under law to equal validity under God. It is a cultural axiom that it does not matter what you believe as long as you believe it sincerely. This cultural viewpoint is on a collision course with biblical Christianity. It denies the doctrine of justification by faith because it denies the necessary object of that faith. It denies the uniqueness of Christ and of the gospel itself.

In his exposition of the gospel in Romans, Paul devotes an entire chapter to grounding the doctrine of justification by faith in the Old Testament, referring to David and Abraham as his prime examples (Romans 4).

Article 5 denies that Old Testament believers lacked any knowledge of the gospel. While expounding Abraham's justification by faith, Paul declares: ". . . it is of faith that it might be according to grace, so that the promise might be sure to all the seed, not only to those who are of the law, but also to those who are of the faith of Abraham, who is the father of us all (as it is written, 'I have made you a father of many nations'). . . ." (Rom. 4:16–17)

Old Testament saints were justified by faith just as we are. Their faith was in the gospel's promise; our faith is in the gospel's fulfillment. They looked forward to Christ; we look backward to him. But the object of saving faith is the same: Christ and his redeeming work.

The Divine Word

> 6. We affirm that faith in Jesus Christ as the divine Word (or Logos, John 1:1), the second Person of the Trinity, co-eternal and co-essential with the Father and the Holy Spirit (Heb. 1:3), is foundational to faith in the Gospel. ☐ We deny that any view of Jesus Christ which reduces or rejects his full deity is Gospel faith or will avail to salvation.

One use of the term *gospel* in our language is to refer to the literary form of the first four books of the New Testament. They are called Gospels because they provide a summary of the person and work of Christ, substantially in narrative form.

The gospel includes at its heart content regarding the person of Christ as well as his work. As we have noted, Christ's person is revealed in and through his work, and his work in its efficacy is defined in large measure by his person. To place one's faith in the gospel is to place one's faith in Christ as the God-man. If he is stripped of his deity, the gospel is fractured.

The first part of article 6 affirms that Christ is the eternal Logos, an affirmation resting on the opening verses of John's Gospel. John's introduction of the Logos concept provided the dominant focus of the church's Christology for the first three centuries. John asserts remarkable things when he says: "In the beginning was the Word *(Logos),* and the Word was with God, and the Word was God. He was in the beginning with God." (John 1:1–2)

John states that the Word or Logos was with God. This assertion distinguishes between the Logos and God, inasmuch as it says one was with the other. In the very next statement John asserts that the Logos was God, indicating an identification of the Logos with God himself.

Early on, this raised the obvious question: How can the Logos be both distinguished from God and identified with him? Attempts to answer this question culminated in the church's formulation of the doctrine of the Trinity, according to which the members of the Godhead are identical in substance or being, while distinguished as persons or subsistences.

John also says the Logos "became flesh and dwelt among us, and we beheld His glory, the glory as of the only begotten of the Father, full of grace and truth" (John 1:14). John's use of the term *Logos* to refer to the pre-existent and eternal Christ is remarkable. The common meaning of the Greek term is simply "word." But because *logos* was a loaded term in the history of Greek philosophy, it takes on greater significance. Early Greek philosophers sought the *archē* principle or the ultimate reality that unifies the diversity of human experiences. This principle would explain why the created world is cosmos rather than chaos.

In Greek philosophy the logos was not conceived of in personal terms, but was a more abstract concept to account for order and harmony in the universe. It was the supreme rational principle or "logic" by which all things fit together and cohere.

That John simply borrowed this loaded philosophical term from Greek thinkers is highly doubtful. However aware he may have been of the word's philosophical import, he was still writing from a Hebrew perspective and filled the concept with Jewish content. Nevertheless, we cannot miss the striking parallels between John's use of the term and its function in Greek philosophy, particularly among the pre-Socratics and the Stoics. The most notable parallel is found in this statement by John: "All things were made through Him, and without Him nothing was made that was made. In Him was life, and the life was the light of men." (John 1:3) It is not that the Greeks had a view of creation at all similar to the Jews'. But for some Greeks, especially the Stoics, there was a "life principle" or a "source of light" in the logos. Stoics affirmed the *logos spermatikos,* or the seminal word or "fire," in which all things contain a "spark." For Stoics the logos is also a source of light in the sense of rational knowledge.

In John's case the Logos, the cosmic Christ, is the Creator of the world, a role reserved in Judaism for God alone. In creation God creates all things, according to John, through the Logos.

The phrase "and the Word was God" (John 1:1) is one of the clearest assertions of the deity of Christ found in Scripture. Jehovah's Witnesses and Mormons deny Christ's deity by arguing that the absence of the definite article ("God" instead of "the God") indicates John was asserting only that the Logos was "a god." John could not possibly have meant to say that Jesus (the Logos) is "a god" because Judaism categorically rejected polytheism. Greek syntax does not require the definite article for the text to convey an identity between the Logos and God. The Mormon and Jehovah's Witness treatment of the text is an exercise in exegetical futility and cannot be taken seriously.

In the early centuries more formidable alternatives to the trinitarian interpretation of John 1:1 came under the guise of the Sabellian heresy and later the Arian heresy, which culminated in the Council of Nicea and the Nicene Creed. These twin heresies proposed two different types of monarchianism.

The term *monarchianism* comes from the prefix *mono,* which means "one," and the root *archē,* which means "beginning, chief, or ruler." The root comes into English as *arch,* in such words as *archenemy, archbishops,* and *archangel.* Monarchianism was driven by the desire to maintain monotheism, which some thought was threatened by trinitarianism. There were two distinct types of monarchianism, *modalistic* and *dynamic.*

The chief exponent of modalistic monarchianism was Sabellius. Following ideas common to Gnosticism and neo-Platonism, Sabellius viewed God as a single essence who emanated from himself different levels or "modes" of being. The highest level was pure spirit, and the farther away from the source of being, the more material things became. Like ripples on a pond, the farthest ripples are the least "pure." Sabellius used the analogy of the sun with its rays to describe God's relationship to the Logos. A sunbeam shares a common essence with the sun, yet can be distinguished from it. In this manner Sabellius used a term that became one of the most controversial terms in Christian history: *homo-ousios,* the Greek term for "same essence" or "same substance." For Sabellius the Logos was *homo-ousios* (of the same essence) with God, but was not God. In A.D. 267 the church denounced Sabellius as a heretic and rejected the term *homo-ousios.*

At the beginning of the fourth century, the church faced a new heresy, dynamic monarchianism, sometimes referred to as adoptionism. Following Lucian and Paul of Samosata, Arius developed the theory that the Logos was the first made and most exalted creature, who in turn created the world and became joined to the human, Jesus. Arius took his cue from New Testament references to Jesus as the "first-born" of all creation and to his being begotten of the Father. In Greek the verb used for "begotten" means "to be, become, or happen," and it is used to describe things that are generated in time and consequently have a beginning.

In Arius's view Jesus "became" the Son of God by virtue of his unity in purpose with the Father. He was "adopted" into the "Godhead" (hence the dynamic change). To express this, Arius used the term *homoi-ousios,* which means "like-substance" or "similar substance."

Arius was condemned at the Council of Nicea, at which the Nicene Creed was formulated. This creed says that Jesus is co-eternal and co-substantial, that he was "begotten, not made." Two things are striking here. First, the church understood the biblical idea of "begottenness" in terms of status, not biological or creaturely origin. Second, the church reversed its position regarding the term *homo-ousios.* While the previous synod at Antioch had denied *homo-ousios* as used by Sabellius, the

Council of Nicea now insisted on it as an expression of trinitarian orthodoxy. Though at first glance the two decisions appear to be contradictory, under closer examination it becomes clear they were not. At both Antioch and Nicea, the church wished to affirm the full deity of Christ. Sabellius had denied Christ's deity by his use of *homo-ousios.* Arius had denied Christ's deity by his use of *homoi-ousios.*

The church saw the Arian heresy as such a great threat to trinitarianism that she was willing to use a term that had earlier been misused in a modalistic way in order to counter Arianism. The church did not retreat to modalism—the Sabellian heresy had largely faded by this time. The church rejected both modalistic and dynamic monarchianism in favor of trinitarianism, which saw the members of the Godhead as one in essence and as all co-eternal. In this context the church sang the Gloria Patri: "Glory be to the Father, and to the Son, and to the Holy Ghost: as it was in the beginning, is now and ever shall be, world without end. Amen."

Again in the fifth century the doctrine of the Trinity came under attack by the twin heresies of Nestorianism and Eutychianism (the monophysite heresy) that culminated in the Ecumenical Council of Chalcedon in 451. The monophysite heresy articulated by Eutyches taught that Christ had only one *(mono-)* nature *(physis).* This single nature was "theanthropic," a word coming from the Greek words for God *(Theos)* and man *(anthropos).* Jesus' single nature was neither truly human nor truly divine, but a mixture or blend of deity and humanity. Nestorius argued that if Jesus had two natures, he must have had two personalities or been two persons. For Nestorius the divine and human natures of Christ were separated or divided.

In condemning both Eutyches and Nestorius, the Council of Chalcedon clearly affirmed the dual nature of Christ: he is *vere homo* (truly man) and *vere Deus* (truly God). Added to this positive affirmation about the two natures of Christ were the famous four negatives of Chalcedon—these two natures, in perfect union, were *without mixture, confusion, separation,* or *division.* Each nature retained its own attributes.

At Chalcedon the church set the borders for speculating about the two natures of Christ. The unity of two distinct natures, human and divine, was affirmed and guarded by the negatives, lest we blur their distinctions by mixing or confusing them, or destroy their unity by separating or dividing them. The church insisted that we distinguish between the two natures without dividing them.

With respect to the Trinity and the person of Christ, the questions of essence and person are paramount. The church confesses that God is one in essence but three in person, and that Christ is one in person and two in essence (or nature).

In the scope of Christian history, there have been four centuries in which the deity of Christ has come under serious attack: the fourth, fifth, nineteenth, and twentieth centuries. It is important to note that with the advent of nineteenth-century liberalism the doctrine of Christ's deity came under strong attack from within the visible church. That attack has continued with vehemence throughout the twentieth century. Historic Christian orthodoxy, however, maintains the deity of Christ as essential to the Christian faith and the biblical gospel. A denial of Christ's deity is the essence of unbelief.

Article 6 denies that a "faith" that lacks the deity of Christ is a saving faith and will avail to salvation.

Truly Human

> 7. We affirm that Jesus Christ is God incarnate (John 1:14). The virgin-born descendant of David (Rom. 1:3), he had a true human nature, was subject to the Law of God (Gal. 4:5), and was like us at all points, except without sin (Heb. 2:17, 7:26–28). We affirm that faith in the true humanity of Christ is essential to faith in the Gospel. ☐ We deny that anyone who rejects the humanity of Christ, his incarnation, or his sinlessness, or who maintains that these truths are not essential to the Gospel, will be saved (1 John 4:2–3).

Orthodox Christianity affirms not only that Christ is truly God *(vere Deus)* but that he is truly man *(vere homo)*. As our mediator he is the God-man who enters into our full humanity. He is the new Adam who does for us what the first Adam failed to do.

The apostolic preaching *(kērygma)* included manifold references to Christ in his perfect humanity. This man was of the seed of David, from the tribe of Judah. Though miraculously conceived by the Holy Spirit, he was nevertheless born of a woman.

An eternal Logos posed no inherent problem to Greek philosophy. But that the spiritual Logos could become incarnate was unthinkable to the Greek mind. In Plato's philosophy the material world (the world of the receptacle) is the world of inherent imperfection. Only the pure being of the "ideal" can be free of imperfection. In human terms Greeks viewed the physical body as the prison of the soul. For them redemption means the release of the soul from its bodily captivity, so that redemption is *from* the body.

For the Jew the physical realm of nature, including the human body, is part of the good creation of God that received his divine benediction. The goal of creation is not the destruction of the physical world, but its renovation. This world is now in a fallen state, but that state is not its intrinsically necessary condition, as in Greek or Gnostic thought. The Apostles' Creed affirms the resurrection of the body *(resurrectionis carnis),* a reference not to Christ's resurrection body but to ours.

For the Christian, redemption is not *from* the body but *of* the body. We look forward to a perfected humanity that will participate in the glorified humanity evidenced in Christ. Paul declares to the Corinthians: ". . . now Christ is risen from the dead, and has become the firstfruits of those who have fallen asleep. For since by man came death, by Man also came the resurrection of the dead. For as in Adam all die, even so in Christ all shall be made alive." (1 Cor. 15:20–22) Later Paul elaborates:

> The body is sown in corruption, it is raised in incorruption. It is sown in dishonor, it is raised in glory. It is sown in weakness, it is raised in power. It is sown a natural body, it is raised a spiritual body. There is a natural body, and there is a spiritual body. And so it is written, "The first man Adam became a living being."

> The last Adam became a life-giving spirit. However, the spiritual is not first, but the natural, and afterward the spiritual. The first man was of the earth, made of dust; the second Man is the Lord from heaven. As was the man of dust, so also are those who are made of dust; and as is the heavenly Man, so also are those who are heavenly. And as we have borne the image of the man of dust, we shall also bear the image of the heavenly Man. (1 Cor. 15:42–49)

Paul dramatically ties the humanity of Christ to our redemption. To be sure, Paul speaks of Christ as a heavenly man in contrast to a man of dust. Yet as heavenly as he is, Christ is still a man.

The true humanity of Jesus was deemed an essential part of the biblical gospel by John in his first epistle. He writes concerning the Antichrist: "Little children, it is the last hour; and as you have heard that the Antichrist is coming, even now many antichrists have come, by which we know that it is the last hour. They went out from us, but they were not of us; for if they had been of us, they would have continued with us; but they went out that they might be made manifest, that none of them were of us." (1 John 2:18–19)

Later in the epistle John gives more information concerning the spirit of the Antichrist: "Beloved, do not believe every spirit, but test the spirits, whether they are of God; because many false prophets have gone out into the world. By this you know the Spirit of God: Every spirit that confesses that Jesus Christ has come in the flesh is of God, and every spirit that does not confess that Jesus Christ has come in the flesh is not of God. And this is the spirit of the Antichrist, which you have heard was coming, and is now already in the world." (1 John 4:1–3)

Note that a chief characteristic of the spirit of Antichrist is the denial that Jesus Christ has come in the flesh. John was almost certainly combating the heresy of docetism. Docetists are usually considered a subgroup of an early form of Gnosticism. The term *docetism* comes from the Greek verb *dokein,* which means "to think, seem, or appear." Docetists, influenced by Greek philosophy and Oriental dualism, could not abide the idea that God would contaminate his pure spirituality by uniting himself with a real, physical human nature. This was a stumbling block, an offense to their thinking.

Docetists were well aware of the apostolic witness to Christ's human nature, by which he manifested himself in a body and was given to hunger, thirst, and weariness. Docetists said that, though Jesus "seemed" or "appeared" to have a body of flesh, he did not really possess such a nature. His body was merely an illusory phantom—an outward manifestation ungrounded in real corporeality. Hence the term *docetism,* indicating a mere semblance of flesh without the reality of flesh.

This view was regarded as of the spirit of Antichrist, and it was one of the earliest heresies rejected by the apostolic church.

Tied to his human nature, his role as Mediator, and his identity as the second Adam is the sinlessness of Christ. To effect our salvation, Jesus had to obey the law of God in every respect. He had to be morally perfect to qualify for his atoning work. He was called to be the Lamb of God *(Agnus Dei),* the lamb without blemish. The author of Hebrews said he "was in all points tempted as we are, yet without sin" (Heb. 4:15). Christ was the one who, though he knew no sin, became sin for us.

Recently I heard a seminary professor refer to a woman as "an evangelical scholar" who protested Jesus' remarks to the Syro-Phoenician woman. By implication Jesus called her a dog. His remarks were not only insensitive, according to the woman scholar, but abusive and demeaning. This feminist was indicting Jesus with sin. What bothered me about this report was not only that the scholar was so critical of Jesus' behavior, but that the professor had referred to her as an "Evangelical." How can a person deny the sinlessness of Jesus and still be called an Evangelical?

Article 7's denial makes the point that Christ's full humanity, his incarnation, and his sinlessness are all essential to the gospel and are therefore essential to authentic Evangelicalism.

A persistent danger manifests itself within evangelical circles to move, by reaction, to the opposite error of that of liberalism. Liberalism denies the deity of Christ. It affirms his humanity to the exclusion of his deity, so that his deity is swallowed up by his humanity.

Historically Evangelicals have been so zealous to preserve the deity of Christ that they have tended to neglect or even negate his true humanity. Sometimes we see Jesus in terms of a deified humanity, in which the true limits of his humanity are swallowed up by his deity. Subtle forms of the monophysite heresy invade the church in every generation, subtleties that endanger the reality of Jesus' humanity and thereby the purity of the gospel.

The Gospel of Jesus Christ: Part 3

8. We affirm that the atonement of Christ is an essential element of the gospel.
9. We affirm that Christ's saving work included both his life and his death on our behalf.
10. We affirm that the bodily resurrection of Christ from the dead is essential to the biblical gospel.

Christ the Perfect Sacrifice

From the divine and human natures of Christ, *The Gospel of Jesus Christ* moves to his work of atonement, affirming that Christ not only died for us, but also lived for us.

Christ's Atonement

> 8. We affirm that the atonement of Christ by which, in his obedience, he offered a perfect sacrifice, propitiating the Father by paying for our sins and satisfying divine justice on our behalf according to God's eternal plan, is an essential element of the Gospel. ☐ We deny that any view of the Atonement that rejects the substitutionary satisfaction of divine justice, accomplished vicariously for believers, is compatible with the teaching of the Gospel.

So central is the atonement to the biblical gospel that the Apostle Paul resolved to know nothing but Christ and him crucified. The passion of Jesus fills a large measure of the Gospel record and is the subject of much of the apostolic teaching regarding his work.

The biblical language used to interpret the meaning and significance of the cross is rich and varied. Many strands are woven together in the biblical concept of the atonement.

Historically many theories have been preferred to explain the cross, some of which clearly reject that Christ died to satisfy divine justice. One of these is the "moral influence" view of the atonement, which teaches that Christ functions as an example to us of the importance of obeying the law and upholding the government of God.

That Christ is the supreme moral example is not in question. The issue is, Did he do more than serve as an example or influence? To this the Scriptures universally reply in the affirmative. His death on the cross is a cosmic event of reconciliation.

Was the satisfaction of God's justice required out of a natural necessity, or was it merely the means God chose due to his pact with mankind? The Socinian heresy denied that satisfaction was necessary at all, claiming that God both could and would gratuitously forgive sin without requiring any payment or satisfaction for it.

Orthodox theologians argue that satisfaction is demanded at least insofar as God has decreed it. Some believe he could have chosen another method, but once he did decree it, then it was required. The common view of the church is that God decreed the necessity of satisfaction because it was a natural and absolute requirement for him to maintain his own justice. Having his justice satisfied by a substitute, who is punished in our place, reveals both God's justice and his grace. In one act he is both the Just and the Justifier. In the cross he does not compromise his own righteousness, nor does he negotiate his own justice. Sin is truly punished in Christ's atonement. Christ is the propitiation for our sins.

The Bible uses the terms *propitiation* and *expiation*. The two terms differ in their prefixes and their meaning. The prefix *pro* means "before" or "in front of." Propitiation refers to the vertical direction of the sacrifice of Christ. It is an act directed toward the Father, before whom Christ makes satisfaction for our sins. The prefix *ex* means "from" or "out of." In his work of expiation, Christ removes our sins from us, in a horizontal direction. Our sins are "remitted" or "sent away from us."

Both expiation and propitiation were prefigured in the Old Testament drama of the Day of Atonement. Three animals were used in the ceremony, a bull and two goats. The bull is used first as a sin offering for the high priest and his house. The first goat is slain on behalf of the people, and its blood is sprinkled on the mercy seat, symbolizing the act of propitiation.

The second goat is the scapegoat. The law in Leviticus reads: ". . . when he has made an end of atoning for the Holy Place, the tabernacle of meeting, and the altar, he shall bring the live goat; and Aaron shall lay both his hands on the head of the live goat, confess over it all the iniquities of the children of Israel, and all their transgressions, concerning all their sins, putting them on the head of the goat, and shall send it away into the wilderness by the hand of a suitable man. The goat shall bear on itself all their iniquities to an uninhabited land; and he shall release the goat in the wilderness." (Lev. 16:20–22)

In the ceremony of the scapegoat, we see the drama of expiation via a substitute, or what we may call "vicarious expiation." In laying on his hands, Aaron symbolizes the transfer of the people's sins to the back of the goat. Now, by virtue of imputation, the goat bears the people's sins. The goat is sent away, indicating the removal or remission of sin via expiation.

It is vitally important that the goat is sent outside the camp into uninhabited wilderness. This action must be understood in light of the sanctions established in the Mosaic covenant. In Deuteronomy God promises a blessing to all who obey his commandments, blessing in the city and the country, in their produce and livestock, in all areas of their lives: ". . . it shall come to pass, if you diligently obey the voice of the LORD your God, to observe carefully all His commandments which I command you today, that the LORD your God will set you high above all nations of the earth. And all these blessings shall come upon you and overtake you, because you obey the voice of the LORD your God. . . ." (Deut. 28:1–2)

In like manner God promises a negative sanction, a curse, on all who violate his commandments, a curse that will strike in city and country, in farm and field, and in all things: "... it shall come to pass, if you do not obey the voice of the LORD your God, to observe carefully all His commandments and His statutes which I command you today, that all these curses will come upon you and overtake you. ..." (Deut. 28:15).

To understand the language of blessing and curse, let us examine the classic Hebrew benediction: "The LORD bless you and keep you; the LORD make His face shine upon you, and be gracious to you; the LORD lift up His countenance upon you, and give you peace" (Num. 6:24–26).

The literary form of the benediction is a type of synonymous parallelism in which each verse repeats the same thought using different words. In each verse there are two related benefits. It looks like this:

Bless . . . keep
Make His face shine . . . be gracious
Lift up His countenance . . . give peace

"Keeping," "being gracious," and "giving peace" are parallel concepts. Likewise "bless," "make His face shine," and "lift up his countenance" are parallel. To the Jew the highest possible state of blessedness is the beatific vision—being able to see the face of God. The closer one comes to seeing his face, the higher the degree of felicity. Blessedness is inseparably related to God's nearness.

The antithesis of blessing is curse. To fall under the curse is to be not "kept" or "preserved" by God. It is to experience not his grace, but his justice. It is to have not peace (shalom) but conflict. To be cursed is to be removed from his presence, to be forbidden ever to see his face, to be cast into outer darkness where the light of his countenance does not shine.

In the New Testament Paul speaks of Christ's bearing the curse of the law on behalf of his people: "Christ has redeemed us from the curse of the law, having become a curse for us (for it is written, 'Cursed is everyone who hangs on a tree'), that the blessing of Abraham might come upon the Gentiles in Christ Jesus, that we might receive the promise of the Spirit through faith" (Gal. 3:13–14).

The drama of the curse is played out in detail in the Gospel narratives of the crucifixion. Christ is delivered first to the Gentiles for judgment. He is killed according to Roman law by "hanging on a tree." It becomes dark in the middle of the afternoon, and Christ cries out about being forsaken. All of these elements reenact the driving of the scapegoat outside the camp, its banishment to the outer darkness.

By his passive obedience Christ receives the curse due to us. The curse is punishment for the sin that has been imputed to him. "Passive obedience" means the things Jesus allowed to happen to him for our sake. He accepts the dreadful cup the Father sets before him and drinks it to its bitter dregs. He passively endures the punishment for sin that is not his own, but is transferred to him by imputation. He fulfills the role of the Suffering Servant of Isaiah 53: "Surely He has borne our griefs and carried our sorrows; yet we esteemed Him stricken, smitten by God, and afflicted. But He was wounded for our transgressions, He was bruised for our iniquities; the chastisement for our peace was upon Him, and by His stripes we are healed." (Isa. 53:4–5)

There is a litany of substitution here that cannot be missed, a repeated contrast between "he" and "our." Christ is smitten by God. It pleases God to bruise him as he exacts satisfaction from Christ for our sin. Satisfaction and substitution are essential to the atonement, and without them there is no gospel and no evangelical faith.

Christ's Life and Death

> 9. We affirm that Christ's saving work included both his life and his death on our behalf (Gal. 3:13). We declare that faith in the perfect obedience of Christ by which he fulfilled all the demands of the Law of God in our behalf is essential to the Gospel. ☐ We deny that our salvation was achieved merely or exclusively by the death of Christ without reference to his life of perfect righteousness.

On the cross, Christ took upon himself the negative sanction of the law, becoming a curse for us. Satisfying the curse does not in itself guarantee the blessing. For the positive sanction of the blessing, the law must be obeyed. This is a vitally important element of Christ's vicarious work. He is our substitute not only in death, but in life. He satisfies not only the punitive demands of God's justice, but also those demands required for the blessing. In this respect Christ not only takes on himself our demerits, but also merits the blessing for us by his perfect obedience. He is not only our curse, but also our righteousness.

By his "active obedience" is meant Christ's positive actions by which he submits himself to the law in every respect, fulfilling it actively in his own obedience. His meat and drink were to do the will of the Father. His work as the second Adam is to be that man whose righteousness makes us alive.

We see this obedience in Jesus' baptism. When Jesus presents himself to John the Baptist to submit to this new cleansing rite God has required of his people, John is reluctant to baptize Jesus. John has already declared Jesus to be the Lamb of God. Matthew gives this account: "Then Jesus came from Galilee to John at the Jordan to be baptized by him. And John tried to prevent Him, saying, 'I have need to be baptized by You, and are You coming to me?' But Jesus answered and said to him, 'Permit it to be so now, for thus it is fitting for us to fulfill all righteousness.' Then [John] allowed Him." (Matt. 3:13–15)

It was unthinkable to John that Jesus should be baptized since this rite calls for acknowledgment of sin and for repentance. If Jesus was baptized, then Jesus would be regarded as a sinner and could not qualify as the Lamb without blemish. Jesus instructed John, in somewhat cryptic terms, to do it anyway. Jesus did not give John a full-orbed theological explanation for his action, telling John only that it is "fitting" or "necessary" that it be done. Why? To "fulfill all righteousness." This phrase can only mean that it was necessary for Jesus to obey the law of God and his righteousness at every point, including this new mandate God had given to Israel.

In his role as Messiah, Jesus was the Servant of the Lord who took it upon himself to fulfill all the commands God had imposed on his covenant people, Israel. From the beginning of his life to its end, Jesus submitted at every point to the law. He was circumcised after eight days and presented to God in the temple after the days of Mary's purification were completed.

The life of Jesus is recorded for us in the book we call the New Testament. But his entire life, up to the point of his death, took place in the period of redemptive history we call the Old Testament or the Old Covenant. Jesus indicated that the Law and the Prophets rule up to (and including) John. We read of John the Baptist in the New Testament, but in redemptive terms he belongs to the Old Testament period. The Old Covenant reigns up to the point when the New Covenant is inaugurated. That takes place in the upper room during the Last Supper, when Jesus declares the New Covenant in his blood, a covenant he ratified the next day on the cross.

So throughout his life Jesus was busy living under the terms of the Old Testament. In this regard we see that his obedience is both passive and active. It has a two-fold effect: satisfactory and meritorious. He provides for us both escape from hell and entrance into heaven.

Paul draws a contrast between Adam and Christ, between disobedience and obedience and their consequences for those represented. Adam, by his trespass, failed to win the blessing for himself and those whom he represented. Christ, by his obedience, wins the blessing of God not only for himself, but also for his people (Rom. 5:19). Paul remarks: ". . . what the law could not do in that it was weak through the flesh, God did by sending His own Son in the likeness of sinful flesh, on account of sin: He condemned sin in the flesh, that the righteous requirement of the law might be fulfilled in us. . . ." (Rom. 8:3–4).

We have become "the righteousness of God in Him" (2 Cor. 5:21) because he is our righteousness.

The denial of article 9 reinforces that both the death of Christ and his life have salvific value. Both are essential to the full redemption Christ has achieved for us.

Christ's Resurrection

10. We affirm that the bodily resurrection of Christ from the dead is essential to the biblical Gospel (1 Cor. 15:14). ☐ We deny the validity

of any so called gospel that denies the historical reality of the bodily resurrection of Christ.

Though the idea of a resurrectionless Christianity is not a new one, it has gained momentum in the past two centuries. Nineteenth-century liberalism, in the aftermath of the Enlightenment, sought to redefine Christianity in terms of values and ethics within the limits of natural reason. Miracles of every sort, as reported in the Bible, were revised to fit the paradigm of a closed, mechanistic universe, operating according to inherent, fixed, natural laws. The laws of biology precluded such things as virgin births and resurrections. What Emil Brunner called simply "unbelief" was expressed in a deconstructed and revised understanding of Christian "faith."

The biblical record was interpreted according to naturalism, and historical-narrative passages were recast in symbolic or poetic terms. For example, the feeding of five thousand was explained in terms of an "ethical" miracle. Jesus, by example and pedagogy, persuaded those who had brought food for themselves to share these provisions with those who had none. The value of compassionate humanitarianism becomes the story's true "miracle."

A popular view of the resurrection in the nineteenth century was the so-called "swoon theory": Jesus never really died, he simply fell into a coma. His heartbeat was so weak that there were no discernable signs of life, leading his would-be executioners to think he had expired. So they gave his body to his followers to be buried in a tomb owned by Joseph of Arimathea. They anointed his body with spices and wrapped it in linen. The combination of these dressings and the tomb's coolness revived him from his coma-like swoon. How was he able to get out of the grave wrappings and roll away the stone? His friends helped him. This theory, then, describes not resurrection, but resuscitation.

Though the swoon theory sounds far-fetched, documented cases of people thought to be dead suddenly awakening to consciousness on the slab of a morgue or in the basement of a funeral home makes the theory at least a natural possibility. Following the canons of David Hume, who argued that the radically unlikely must always be preferred to an actual miracle, naturalists argued that the swoon theory is less far-fetched than an actual resurrection. If the universe operates by absolutely fixed internal laws, then resurrection is an *a priori* impossibility.

This view is on a collision course, not only with the resurrection narratives of the New Testament, but also with the entire theological world view of Scripture. The doctrines of creation and providence, axiomatic to Judaeo-Christianity, see the laws of nature, not as fixed or independent, but as subject to the sovereign God, who sustains and governs his creation. It is in him that we live, move, and have our being. The laws of nature are secondary causes that depend for their power and operation on the primary causality of God himself.

A profound difference exists between a naturalistic view of Christ's resurrection and the biblical view. According to naturalism it was impossible for Christ to rise. According to the New Testament it was impossible for him not to rise. Death could not possibly hold him. This impossibility is rooted in the biblical view of death's relationship to sin: Death is a consequence of sin. In the unique case of Jesus, who was sinless, death had no abiding claim upon him. Once his atoning death was acceptable to God as a vicarious offering, God vindicated his Son's perfection and the accomplishment of his Son's atonement by imputation, raising him "for our justification." In theological terms Jesus was raised for his own vindication and for the vindication of our justification.

In the twentieth century Rudolf Bultmann's neo-liberalism made a direct assault on the biblical world view, characterizing it as a primitive, prescientific view of a three-storied universe with heaven above and hell below the plane of this world, a world view encased in the husk of mythology. Bultmann argued that one must be scientifically or philosophically schizophrenic to use the radio, a television, electric lights, and antibiotics and still believe in a world inhabited by demons and angels, a world in which virgin births and resurrections occur. For the modern person the Bible must first be demythologized by the critic, who cuts through the mythological "husk" of the gospel to penetrate its historical core. That core of history is largely restricted to the faith of the early church, and this historical faith must be recast and reinterpreted according to modern categories of existential philosophy. One must ask Bultmann, however, what television and radio have to do with angels, or antibiotics with resurrection? The mere presence of these modern tools says nothing about the theological world view of Scripture.

In the "death of God" movement of the 1960s, Paul Van Buren gave another spin to the resurrection accounts. He argued that the resurrection was a "discernment situation." He noted that the Gospel record places great stress on Jesus' postresurrection appearances. That is, the resurrection of Christ is couched, not in terms of a spiritual or hypothetical possibility (as in Plato's doctrine of immortality), but in terms of testimony by those who claimed to have seen the resurrected Christ with their own eyes.

Van Buren probes this matter of "seeing" the resurrected Christ. In historical narratives recording these sightings, readers commonly understand that when the apostles say they "saw" Jesus, this means Christ fell within the perview of their vision in a sensate manner. That is, the apostles were describing an optical or ocular experience.

But there is another use of the verb *to see*. It often expresses the idea of discernment or understanding. When a difficult concept is explained to me and I finally understand what was once perplexing, I may respond, "Now I see it!" This is not an optical seeing, but an intellectual grasping or seeing. (Note that the word *grasp* also has either a tactile or an intellectual meaning.) It is something akin to what is expressed in the ditty "I see, said the blind man, as he picked up his hammer and saw."

For Van Buren the minds of the disciples were clouded concerning the true meaning of Jesus, particularly his death. On further reflection after his death, they finally came to "see" what Jesus is all about. The resurrection texts, then, are intended to communicate, not a literal visual experience of a man who died and came back to life, but a change in the disciples' perception. The body of Jesus was not changed, but the disciples' understanding of Jesus was.

Such theories were confronted by the apostles in the early church. We see this in Paul's defense of the resurrection in 1 Corinthians 15, where he responds to a view that had penetrated the Corinthian church: There is no resurrection of the dead.

(Whether this view denied only the resurrection of believers or whether it denied the resurrection of anyone, including Jesus, is a matter of debate.)

Paul addresses the issue of employing a form of argument popular in antiquity, the *ad hominem* argument (not the *ad hominem abusive* fallacy): The debater temporarily adopted the stance of his opponent (for the sake of argument), took the argument to its logical conclusion, and thereby revealed its absurdity (the *reductio ad absurdum* form of argument).

Paul adopts the premise "There is no resurrection," then spells out its necessary implications. He argues: ". . . if there is no resurrection of the dead, then Christ is not risen. And if Christ is not risen, then our preaching is vain [empty] and your faith is also vain [empty]. Yes, and we are found false witnesses of God, because we have testified of God that He raised up Christ, whom He did not raise up—if in fact the dead do not rise. For if the dead do not rise, then Christ is not risen. And if Christ is not risen, your faith is futile; you are still in your sins! Then also those who have fallen asleep in Christ have perished. If in this life only we have hope in Christ, we are of all men the most pitiable." (1 Cor. 15:13–19)

Paul reasons that the premise (there is no resurrection of the dead) flows to his conclusions, not by merely possible inference, but by necessary inference. The conclusions flow by resistless logic. For Paul Christianity without resurrection is irrational and illogical and ultimately an exercise in futility.

Paul does not rest his case for the resurrection on the grounds that its denial leads to hopelessness or futility. He does not argue that we should affirm the resurrection simply because the alternatives are grim. He rests his case on the basis of biblical prophecy and eyewitness testimony, including his own. His *ad hominem* argument does demonstrate, however, that the resurrection is essential to Christian faith. He demonstrates that the resurrection of Christ is a *sine qua non* of the gospel.

In this respect Paul confirms the denial of article 10: Any "gospel" that denies the reality of the historical resurrection of Christ is invalid.

The Gospel of Jesus Christ: Part 4

11. We affirm that the biblical doctrine of justification by faith alone in Christ alone is essential to the gospel.
12. We affirm that the doctrine of imputation is essential to the biblical gospel.
13. We affirm that the righteousness of Christ, which is imputed to us by the forensic declaration of God, is the sole ground of our justification.
14. We affirm that God declares us just, remits our sins, and adopts us as his children, by his grace alone, and through faith alone, because of Christ alone, while we are still sinners.
15. We affirm that saving faith results in sanctification.

10

The Righteousness of Christ

The gospel not only encompasses a summary of the person and work of Christ, but also includes the manner in which the believer appropriates the benefits of Christ's work. That these benefits are received by faith alone is an essential part of the good news.

Justification by Faith Alone

> 11. We affirm that the biblical doctrine of justification by faith alone in Christ alone is essential to the Gospel (Rom. 3:28; 4:5; Gal. 2:16). □ We deny that any person can believe the biblical Gospel and at the same time reject the apostolic teaching of justification by faith alone in Christ alone. We also deny that there is more than one true Gospel (Gal. 1:6–9).

Article 11 affirms not only that *sola fide* is true but that this doctrine is an essential element of the gospel itself. That *sola fide* is integral to the gospel is clear in Paul's exposition of the gospel in Romans. New Testament scholars usually agree that the thematic statement for the Epistle to the Romans is found in chapter 1: ". . . I am not ashamed of the gospel of Christ, for it is the power of God to salvation for everyone who believes, for the Jew first and also for the Greek. For in it the righteousness of God is revealed from faith to faith; as it is written, 'The just shall live by faith.'" (Rom. 1:16–17)

In chapters 3 and 4 Paul gives a detailed exposition of his doctrine of justification, which is inseparably linked to the gospel. He writes that all who believe are "justified freely by His grace through the redemption that is in Christ Jesus, whom God set forth to be a propitiation by His blood, through faith, to demonstrate His righteousness . . . that [God] might be just and the justifier of the one who has faith in Jesus" (Rom. 3:24–26).

Here Paul teaches that we receive the benefits of Christ's propitiation for our sins by faith alone, and not by works. This is seen first in chapter 3: "Therefore we conclude that a man is justified by faith apart from the deeds of the law" (Rom. 3:28). This is further seen in chapter 4, where Abraham is the prototype of those who are justified by faith alone and are counted righteous the moment faith is present, before any works have followed: ". . . we say that faith was accounted to Abraham for righteousness. How then was it accounted? While he was circumcised, or uncircumcised? Not while circumcised, but while uncircumcised. And he received the sign of circumcision, a seal of the righteousness of the faith which he had while still uncircumcised, that he might be the father of all those who believe. . . ." (Rom. 4:9–11)

Here the apostle elaborates on what he has declared at the beginning of chapter 4: Abraham was justified not by his works but by his faith, and this justification was of grace and not of debt.

Paul also connects *sola fide* to the gospel in an essential way in Galatians: ". . . knowing that a man is not justified by the works of the law but by faith in Jesus Christ, . . . we have believed in Christ Jesus, that we might be justified by faith in Christ and not by the works of the law; for by the works of the law no flesh shall be justified" (Gal. 2:16).

Paul is not saying that we are not justified by works alone and that faith too is necessary. He is eliminating works of the law altogether from the ground of our justification. He is not teaching that we are justified by faith plus works since, as he declared in Romans, we are justified by faith "apart from" works. The phrase "apart from" confirms the *sola* in *sola fide.*

Again, that *sola fide* is essential to the gospel is seen in the first chapter of Galatians when Paul warns against perverting the true gospel: "I marvel that you are turning away so soon from Him who called you in the grace of Christ, to a different gospel, which is not another; but there are some who trouble you and want to pervert the gospel of Christ. But even if we, or an angel from heaven, preach any other gospel to you than what we have preached to you, let him be accursed. As we have said before, so now I say again, if anyone preaches any other gospel to you than what you have received, let him be accursed." (Gal. 1:6–9) That Paul was encountering the Judaizer heresy in Galatians is hardly in question. This heresy involved the adding of works to faith as a necessary condition for justification. The Judaziers were denying that justification is by faith alone. Such a denial the apostle saw as a perversion of the gospel, a gospel different from what the apostles preached, a gospel that is really not another gospel because there can be no other gospel. There is only one true gospel, and that is the gospel of grace through faith.

It is crystal clear in this context that Paul views the question of how the benefits of Christ's work are appropriated to be a matter bearing on the very essence of the gospel. To pervert the way in which these benefits are received is to pervert the gospel itself. It is to proclaim a different gospel, which is not a real gospel at all.

Paul resorts to the most severe rebuke possible by twice pronouncing an anathema, a judgment of damnation, on anyone who preaches such a perversion of the gospel.

Article 11 affirms that *sola fide* is not a secondary or peripheral matter with respect to the gospel, but an essential and necessary element of the true gospel. Without *sola fide,* we do not have the gospel. A gospel lacking *sola fide* is a different or perverted gospel that is not *the* gospel.

Two-Way Imputation

12. We affirm that the doctrine of the imputation (reckoning or counting) both of our sins to Christ and of his righteousness to us, whereby our sins are fully forgiven and we are fully accepted, is essential to the biblical Gospel (2 Cor. 5:19–21). □ We deny that we are justified by the righteousness of Christ infused into us or by any righteousness that is thought to inhere within us.

As we labored in part 2 of this book, article 12 affirms that just as *sola fide* is essential to the gospel, so the concept of imputation is essential to *sola fide*. Of course it follows that imputation is therefore essential to the gospel. Without imputation we do not have the gospel.

The imputation affirmed here is a double imputation. The first part of double imputation relates, as we have seen in the atonement, to the imputation of our sins to Christ. On the cross our sins and guilt are transferred to him. God lays upon our vicarious substitute the transgressions that are properly ours. This transfer of sin and guilt from us to Christ is necessary for our salvation. Christ, who knew no sin, bore God's wrath not for his own sin (since he had none) but for our sins. His atonement was not made *for* himself, though it was made *by* himself.

We are neither qualified to atone for our sins nor capable of atoning for them. We are debtors who lack the means to pay our debts. God requires perfect obedience from his creatures. If we sin just once, we fall forever short of that standard. Once imperfect we can never regain perfection.

According to a popular expression, "Everybody is entitled to one mistake." This moral entitlement program is nowhere in Scripture. God never gives us a title to sin. Of course, though it remains a condition contrary to fact, if God were indeed to entitle each of us to one sin, we would have used up that entitlement long ago.

If an atonement is to be made for our sins and if we are neither capable of making it nor qualified to make it, then, manifestly, it can be done only via the route of imputation. If Jesus' sacrifice is for us, then its value is counted to or reckoned in our behalf, or its application is transferred to our account. This is precisely what imputation means.

The second part of double imputation is the legal transfer or reckoning of Christ's righteousness to us. This aspect of justification was central to the sixteenth-century Reformation controversy over justification. The idea that we are counted or deemed righteous by God through faith is seen clearly in Genesis 15. When making his covenant promise to the patriarch Abraham, God said: "Do not be afraid, Abram. I am your shield, your exceedingly great reward." (Gen. 15:1) After God explained to Abraham the content of this reward, we read: "And he believed in the LORD, and He accounted it to him for righteousness" (15:6).

This is the text Paul refers to in Romans 4: "What then shall we say that Abraham our father has found according to the flesh? For if Abraham was justified by works, he has something of which to boast, but not before God. For what does the Scripture say? 'Abraham believed God, and it was accounted to him for righteousness.' Now to him who works, the wages are not counted as grace but as debt." (Rom. 4:1–4)

Paul continues to refer to Abraham, but includes a citation from David: "But to him who does not work but believes on Him who justifies the ungodly, his faith is accounted for righteousness, just as David also describes the blessedness of the man to whom God imputes righteousness apart from works: 'Blessed are those whose lawless deeds are forgiven, and whose sins are covered; blessed is the man to whom the LORD shall not impute sin'" (Rom. 4:5–8).

Paul describes the blessedness of the justified person in two distinct ways. First, there is the positive blessing of having someone else's righteousness imputed to the one who has no righteousness of his own. Second, there is the negative blessing of not having one's own sin imputed to him. In the covering and forgiveness of our sins that occur in our justification, not only does God reckon Christ's righteousness to our account, but also God does not count or reckon our own sins against us. This is the very essence of justification.

Later in chapter 4 Paul again returns to the example of Abraham and the citation from Genesis 15: "He did not waver at the promise of God through unbelief, but was strengthened in faith, giving glory to God, and being fully convinced that what He had promised He was also able to perform. And therefore 'it was accounted to him for righteousness.'" (Rom. 4:20–22)

It is clear from Romans 4 that God's promise to Abraham was not limited to matters of descendants or land, but included salvation. This is seen in the following verses: "Now it was not written for his sake alone that it was imputed to him, but also for us. It shall be imputed to us who believe in Him who raised up Jesus our Lord from the dead, who was delivered up because of our offenses, and was raised because of our justification" (Rom. 4:23–25).

Article 12 denies alternate views to imputation as the ground or basis of justification. Specific reference is made to infused or inherent righteousness, concepts that capture the core of Roman Catholicism's historic doctrine of justification. The Council of Trent made infusion and inherent righteousness necessary to the ground of justification. Article 12 distances the evangelical gospel from the Roman Catholic gospel and makes it clear that justification by imputation is a non-negotiable element of the gospel and the evangelical faith.

Here (as in the entire list of affirmations and denials) what is positively believed is set in contrast to what is not believed or affirmed.

Imputed Righteousness

> 13. We affirm that the righteousness of Christ by which we are justified is properly his own, which he achieved apart from us, in and by his perfect obedience. That righteousness is counted, reckoned, or imputed to us by the forensic (that is, legal) declaration of God, as the sole ground of our justification. ☐ We deny that any works we perform at any stage of our existence add to the merit of Christ or earn for us any merit that contributes in any way to the ground of our justification (Gal. 2:16; Eph. 2:8–9; Titus 3:5).

Article 13 confirms what is declared in article 12 and amplifies it. Article 13 begins by affirming that we are justified by the righteousness of Christ. We must remember that the Reformation slogan "justification by faith alone" and the formula *sola fide* are but theological shorthand for the idea that we are justified by Christ alone, whose perfect righteousness and merit are imputed to us by faith alone.

This article stresses the idea that what avails for our justification is not the righteousness of Christ in us, but the righteousness of Christ for us. The righteousness of Christ was performed, not through us, but in his own life of perfect obedience. This is what the magisterial Reformers meant by "alien righteousness" *(iustitium alienum)*. That which is alien is foreign to us or outside of us. It is someone other than we ourselves.

This alien righteousness is the righteousness that belongs properly to Christ and inheres in him. He is the one who earned merit before the Father. He is the one who kept the law perfectly. He is the righteous one. He becomes our righteousness by virtue of God's imputing his righteousness to our account.

This is what Martin Luther meant when he spoke of a righteousness that is *extra nos*. It is a righteousness "outside of us" and "apart from us," meaning the righteousness Christ achieved in his own life. This idea was at the root and core of Luther's formula *simul iustus et peccator*. The justified person is at the same time *(simul)* just or righteous *(justus)* and *(et)* still a sinner *(peccator)*. This means that justification is the justification of the ungodly, who, though already justified by the imputation of Christ's righteousness, are still ungodly to the extent that sin remains in them. The good news is that we do not have to wait until we are inherently righteous before God reckons or counts us as just, remits our sins, and adopts us into his family.

We are counted as just on the ground that Christ's righteousness and merit have been reckoned to us by the legal declaration of God. This is the evangelical doctrine of "forensic" justification.

As the denial of article 13 indicates, the righteousness of Christ is perfect. What is perfect cannot be added to or rendered more perfect. We cannot "increase" in our justification by adding more righteousness or merit to what is already perfect. Neither can we diminish the righteousness or merit that are the ground of our justification. My sin and demerit do not diminish the perfect righteousness and merit of Christ.

The denial does not say that we do no works. As we labored in part 2, true faith always yields the fruit of good works. Faith without works, as James says, is dead. The point is that whatever works we do are never any part of the ground of our justification. The only works that count for our justification are the works of Christ that God accounts to us.

In creation the first Adam was in a state of probation. He was called to obey the commands of the Creator. The penalty for disobedience was death: ". . . the Lord God commanded the man, saying, 'Of every tree of the garden you may freely eat; but of the tree of the knowledge of good and evil you shall not eat, for in the day that you eat of it you shall surely die'" (Gen. 2:16–17).

Later Paul indicates that by one man's sin death reigned over mankind (Rom. 5:17). Adam failed his trial and plunged the world into ruin. Man's relationship to God in creation was based on works. What Adam failed to achieve, Christ, the second Adam, succeeded in achieving. Ultimately the only way one can be justified is by works. We are indeed justified by works, but the works that justify us are the works of the second Adam. To be justified by faith means to be justified by faith in the works of Christ. Our faith is not the ground of our justification. Faith serves as the instrument by which we receive the benefits of the works of Christ, the sole ground of our justification.

Sinners Declared Just

14. We affirm that, while all believers are indwelt by the Holy Spirit and are in the process of being made holy and conformed to the image of Christ, those consequences of justification are not its ground. God declares us just, remits our sins, and adopts us as his children, by his grace alone, and through faith alone, because of Christ alone, while we are still sinners (Rom. 4:5). ☐ We deny that believers must be inherently righteous by virtue of their cooperation with God's life-transforming grace before God will declare them justified in Christ. We are justified while we are still sinners.

Article 14 is chiefly concerned with the order of salvation *(ordo salutis)*, specifically with the relationship between justification and sanctification. The two are indeed connected, as the one (sanctification) flows out of the other (justification). But the two must be distinguished from each other and not confused with each other.

A justified person is always a changed person. A justified person differs from an unjustified person in critical ways. A justified person is a believing person; an unjustified person is an unbelieving person. A justified person is a regenerated person; an unjustified person is an *unregenerate* person. A justified person is *indwelt* by the Holy Spirit; the unjustified person is *not indwelt* by the Holy Spirit. In the justified person the work of sanctification has *begun;* in the unjustified person the work of sanctification has *not begun.*

It is critical to note that, although these changes are present in the justified person, they are not part of the ground of that person's justification. The sole ground of justification remains always and ever the righteousness of Christ.

The changes mentioned are related to our justification, but they are not the meritorious cause of our justification. Some fruit of justification are described by Paul:

> . . . having been justified by faith, we have peace with God through our Lord Jesus Christ, through whom also we have access by faith into this grace in which we stand, and rejoice in hope of the glory of God. And not only that, but we also glory in tribulations, knowing that tribulation produces perseverance; and perseverance, character; and character, hope. Now hope does not disappoint, because the love of God has been poured out in our hearts by the Holy Spirit who was given to us. (Rom. 5:1–5)

The fruit of justification includes peace with God and access to him. Also hope and character are produced within us. We are people who have had the love of God poured out in our hearts because the Holy Spirit has been given to us.

The Holy Spirit dwells in the justified person. By his power we are sanctified or made holy. The goal of sanctification is conformity to the image of Christ. In Ephesians Paul writes: ". . . you He made alive, who were dead in trespasses and sins, in which you once walked according to the course of this world, according to the prince of the power of the air, the spirit who now works in the sons of disobedience, among whom also we all once conducted ourselves in the lusts of our flesh, fulfilling the desires of the flesh and of the mind, and were by nature children of wrath, just as the others" (Eph. 2:1–3).

Here we see the stark contrast between the believer and the unbeliever. The contrast is a matter of life and death, spiritual life and spiritual death. After describing our previous unregenerate condition (Eph. 2:1–3), Paul adds:

> . . . [God] made us alive together with Christ (by grace you have been saved), and raised us up together, and made us sit together in the heavenly places in Christ Jesus, that in the ages to come He might show the exceeding riches of His grace in His kindness toward us in Christ Jesus. For by grace you have been saved through faith, and that not of yourselves; it is the gift of God, not of works, lest anyone should boast. For we are His workmanship, created in Christ Jesus for good works, which God prepared beforehand that we should walk in them. (Eph. 2:5–10)

The goal of our renewal or "quickening" by the Holy Spirit is sanctification. We were created *for* good works. We are not recreated *by* good works, but *for* or *unto* good works. We who are justified by faith are called to walk in love, demonstrating the fruit of the Holy Spirit. The faith that justifies is a faith that works itself out through love (Gal. 5:6).

To be indwelt by the Spirit is to bear the fruit of the Spirit. The apostle declares: ". . . the fruit of the Spirit is love, joy, peace, longsuffering, kindness, goodness, faithfulness, gentleness, self-control. Against such there is no law. And those who are Christ's have crucified the flesh with its passions and desires. If we live in the Spirit, let us also walk in the Spirit." (Gal. 5:22–25)

These elements of sanctification are both the fruit and the evidence of our justification; but they are not the cause or ground of our justification. They are the fruit of those whom God has already declared just and adopted, and whose sins God has already remitted.

Though we distinguish between justification and sanctification, we insist on connecting them in order to evade the pernicious heresy of antinomianism. Antinomians say a person can have true faith and be saved, even while continuing to live a godless life. One can bear no fruit of sanctification, yet remain in a state of grace. The antinomian heresy does more than distinguish between justification and sanctification; it completely divorces them. For the antinomian the justified person may remain an unchanged person. This was repudiated by the Reformation formula that "Justification is by faith alone, but not by a faith that is alone." True faith yields true justification, which in turn yields true sanctification.

Article 14 denies the Roman Catholic doctrine of justification as articulated by the Council of Trent. As we have seen, Trent declared that a person is justified only when and if righteousness inheres in him. Inherent righteousness occurs when a person cooperates with and assents to the grace of justification, which grace is infused into him. In this view God's declaration of justification depends on the believer's prior sanctification. The order of salvation is reversed so that sanctification precedes justification.

This reversal completely vitiates the biblical and evangelical doctrine of justification and turns the gospel from good news to bad. It may be good news to the sinner to hear that he can be saved, but it is bad news in the extreme to hear that he must first achieve inherent righteousness (even with the assistance of grace). If God waits for me to be inherently righteous before declaring me justified, my hope of salvation is crushed. Perhaps the sign over Dante's hell should be placed here: "Abandon hope, all ye who enter here."

Life Transformation

15. We affirm that saving faith results in sanctification, the transformation of life in growing conformity to Christ through the power of the Holy Spirit. Sanctification means ongoing repentance, a life of turning from sin to serve Jesus Christ in grateful reliance on him as one's Lord and Master (Gal. 5:22–25; Rom. 8:4, 13–14). ☐ We reject any view

of justification which divorces it from our sanctifying union with Christ and our increasing conformity to his image through prayer, repentance, cross-bearing, and life in the Spirit.

Historically the relationship between justification and sanctification has been an important issue in the church. Historic Protestantism has viewed sanctification as following justification. Sanctification is the fruit of justification. In justification we are declared righteous while we are still sinners. In sanctification, as we saw in article 14, we are in the process of being made holy and righteous. The progress of sanctification involves both transformation and conformation.

In Romans 12 Paul declares: ". . . do not be conformed to this world, but be transformed by the renewing of your mind. . . ." (Rom. 12:2). In sanctification a kind of spiritual metamorphosis takes place. The Greek word for "form" is *morphos,* from which we derive the name of the science of forms, or *morphology.* This root can have the prefixes (among others) *con* or *trans.* To *conform* is to be "with" the form; to *transform* is to go "across" or "above" the form.

When Paul says we are not to be conformed to the world, he means we are not to be "with" the forms or shapes of this fallen order. Our behavior patterns will not be deemed "normal" in a secular and pagan society. Christians are called to a different form, a higher order of behavior, one that is across or above the normal patterns of paganism. What is normal to fallen humanity is often abnormal to humanity as created and redeemed. In this sense we are called to the ultimate level of nonconformity.

Yet there is a conformity to which we are called, conformity to the image of Christ. In this regard, to be *conformed* we must be *transformed.* By the transforming power of the Holy Spirit, we are moving away from conformity to this world, and toward conformity to Christ.

Though there is no "increase" in our justification, since the ground of it (the righteousness of Christ) can be neither augmented nor diminished, there is increase or "growth" in our sanctification. Sanctification is progressive, seen in our continual repentance and turning from sin. In sanctification believers demonstrate their obedience to their Savior who is also their Lord and Master.

In sanctification we manifest the fruit of the Spirit. The apostle declares: ". . . the fruit of the Spirit is love, joy, peace, long-suffering, kindness, goodness, faithfulness, gentleness, self-control. Against such there is no law. And those who are Christ's have crucified the flesh with its passions and desires. If we live in the Spirit, let us also walk in the Spirit." (Gal. 5:22–25)

The final sentence of article 15 rejects antinomianism and any view that divorces our justification from our sanctifying union with Christ. Again, though it is necessary to distinguish between justification and sanctification to avoid legalism, it is equally necessary to link justification and sanctification to avoid antinomianism.

The Christian life is marked by prayer, repentance, cross-bearing, and life in the Holy Spirit.

The Gospel of Jesus Christ: Part 5

16. We affirm that saving faith includes mental assent to the content of the gospel, acknowledgment of our sin and need, and personal trust and reliance upon Christ and his work.
17. We affirm that, although true doctrine is vital for spiritual health and well-being, we are not saved by doctrine.
18. We affirm that Christ commands his followers to proclaim the gospel to all.

11

Trusting in Christ

With the evangelical insistence that justification is by faith alone, it was imperative in the Reformation, as it is in our day, to understand clearly what constitutes saving faith. Antinomianism is a constant and perennial threat, and it assumes many faces, such as what may be called "easy believism" or "cheap grace."

Saving Faith

16. We affirm that saving faith includes mental assent to the content of the Gospel, acknowledgment of our sin and need, and personal trust and reliance upon Christ and his work. □ We deny that saving faith includes only mental acceptance of the Gospel, and that justification is secured by a mere outward profession of faith. We further deny that any element of saving faith is a meritorious work or earns salvation for us.

Article 16 touches on the historic question regarding the constituent elements of saving faith. Evangelicals and Roman Catholics agree that saving faith includes intellectual acceptance of the content of the gospel. In other words, if the mind rejects the gospel's truth claims, then saving faith cannot be and is not present.

The Reformers delimited three essential elements of saving faith: *notitia* (knowledge of the data or content of the gospel), *assensus* (the intellectual acceptance or assent to the truth of the gospel's content), and *fiducia* (personal reliance on or trust in Christ and his gospel).

These distinctions are taught by Scripture. "You believe that there is one God," writes James. "You do well. Even the demons believe—and tremble!" (James 2:19) Sarcasm virtually drips from James's pen. He compliments those who "believe" in one God, saying that they do well. But what they do so well only qualifies them to be demons. This "well-doing" is accomplished even by Satan and his minions. The demons were among the first to recognize Jesus' true identity. Of a demon-possessed man, we read: ". . . when he saw Jesus from afar, he ran and worshiped Him. And he cried out with a loud voice and said, 'What have I to do with You, Jesus, Son of the Most High God? I implore You by God that You do not torment me.' For [Jesus] said to him, 'Come out of the man, unclean spirit!' Then [Jesus] asked him, 'What is your name?' And he answered, saying, 'My name is Legion; for we are many.' And he begged [Jesus] earnestly that He would not send them out of the country." (Mark 5:6–10)

In the course of this conversation between Jesus and Legion, who inhabited the tormented man, it is clear that the demons recognized Jesus as the "Son of the Most High God." They obviously accepted intellectually the true identity of the person of Christ. They even appealed to God while entreating Jesus not to torment them. But the demons lacked saving faith. They had one of the necessary elements of saving faith but not all of them. Intellectual acceptance is a necessary condition for saving faith, but not a sufficient condition. That is, without intellectual acceptance we cannot be saved, but its mere presence does not bring salvation. Something more is needed to get beyond the level of demons. That something else, according to the Reformers, is *fiducia,* the personal trust in or reliance on Christ, which is notably absent among demons.

It is clear also from the biblical account of Christ's temptation in the wilderness that Satan knew full well whom he was dealing with. To be sure, Satan identified Jesus in questionable terms: "If You are the Son of God, command this stone to become bread" (Luke 4:3). Though Satan referred to Jesus as the Son of God only in hypothetical terms, this does not mean Satan was uncertain about Jesus' identity. Rather Satan was trying to cast doubt in Jesus' mind about the truth of the words he had so recently heard spoken from heaven at his baptism: "You are My beloved Son; in You I am well pleased" (Luke 3:22). Presumably Satan was aware of this divine pronouncement and was convinced of its truth. That Satan intellectually accepted the truth of Christ is the very reason he sought so desperately to defeat Christ. Satan knew who Jesus was, but he hated who Jesus was and was not inclined to place *fiducia* in him.

Article 16 affirms that saving faith includes intellectual acceptance of the gospel's content but is not exhausted by or comprised solely of mental assent.

Article 16 denies that one can have saving faith without intellectual acceptance or assent. This would exclude from salvation even those who call themselves Christians but who at the same time reject essential elements of the gospel. For example, advocates of liberalism or postliberalism who deny Christ's deity, atonement, and resurrection lack one necessary condition of saving faith. As we stated earlier, citing Emil Brunner, no matter how much they admire or respect the man Jesus, or how highly they regard him as a moral model or existential hero, by rejecting his true person and work, they remain in *unbelief.*

This raises the question regarding Roman Catholics who, though they may affirm other essential elements of the gospel, reject *sola fide.* If they do not intellectually accept this element and if this element is essential to the gospel, can they still be saved? The only honest answer I can give to this question is no. This answer raises the hackles of many who seek to affirm unity between Roman Catholics and Evangelicals, and it requires further explanation.

Does this mean that we are saved by the doctrine of *sola fide?* By no means. We are saved by faith in Jesus Christ and his saving work. Mere belief in the doctrine of *sola fide* will save no one. Intellectual acceptance of *sola fide* does not constitute saving faith. The object of *fiducia* must be Christ and his work, not the doctrine of justification. The problem arises when we ask about the consequences of rejecting *sola fide.* If a person rejects *sola fide,* that person rejects an essential element of the gospel. That poses a problem not only at an intellectual or doctrinal level, but at the spiritual level as well. If a person is trusting not in the imputed righteousness of Christ but in his own inherent righteousness, he will not be saved. He lacks a necessary condition of saving faith. In the final analysis he is trusting in another gospel and remains in a state of self-righteousness. By rejecting an essential element of the gospel, he is under the biblical and thus the divine anathema. This is precisely why Martin Luther insisted that *sola fide* is the article by which the church stands or falls. It is the article by which *we* stand or fall.

Is it not possible that there are Roman Catholics who, despite their doctrine, have saving faith? By all means. To actually rely on Christ and his righteousness alone does not mean that one must be able to articulate precisely what is in their minds and hearts. It is not the doctrine of *sola fide* that justifies, but the application of the truth of this doctrine that yields justification. I may be resting completely on Christ and on his work and merit, but I may trip over the formulation of this doctrine.

Two groups of people within the Roman Catholic Church are saved. First, those who consciously, clearly understand and embrace the doctrine of *sola fide* and who possess true saving faith. They may be living a lie by remaining in the Roman Catholic Church for one reason or another (for example, trying to reform their own church from within rather than departing from it). Or they may not understand their church's teaching on justification and have grasped the true gospel by reading Scripture or by hearing the gospel from others.

Second, those who do not fully grasp the gospel but who intuitively understand that their only hope is in Christ and in his work in their behalf and who trust him fully. My guess is that multitudes within the Roman Catholic Church are in this condition.

If a person fully understands *sola fide* and Rome's view of justification and if he rejects *sola fide* and places his trust in the Roman system of salvation, he will perish in his sin because he has not believed the gospel.

On the other hand, article 16 denies that we are justified by a mere profession of faith. There may be multitudes within the evangelical community who intellectually accept *sola fide* and the whole gospel but who have no *fiducia*. They may believe *sola fide* intellectually, but in the final analysis they are relying on their own works or achievements to get them into heaven. They do not have saving faith in the gospel. Jesus warned of those who honor him with their lips while their hearts are far from him. It is by the *possession* of faith, not by its mere *profession*, that we are justified.

True Doctrine

17. We affirm that, although true doctrine is vital for spiritual health and well-being, we are not saved by doctrine. Doctrine is necessary to inform us how we may be saved by Christ, but it is Christ who saves. ☐ We deny that the doctrines of the Gospel can be rejected without harm. Denial of the Gospel brings spiritual ruin and exposes us to God's judgment.

What was expressed in part in article 16 is explicitly reinforced in article 17: It is Christ who saves us, not our doctrine. Here a distinction is made between that which is vital for spiritual health and that which actually saves us. Since we are saved by Christ and his gospel, it is vitally important that we understand correctly who Christ is and what he has accomplished on our behalf. As we saw in article 16, mental assent to the truth of the gospel is necessary, but in itself it cannot save us.

In the denial article 17 speaks to the common sentiment expressed in Christian circles that doctrine is not important. The doctrines of the gospel are so important that they cannot be rejected without harm, indeed harm that is catastrophic. Rejection of the doctrines of the gospel leaves us in a ruined state and under divine judgment.

Personal Testimonies

18. We affirm that Jesus Christ commands his followers to proclaim the Gospel to all living persons, evangelizing everyone everywhere, and discipling believers within the fellowship of the church. A full and faithful witness to Christ includes the witness of personal testimony, godly living, and acts of mercy and charity to our neighbor, without which the preaching of the Gospel appears barren. □ We deny that the witness of personal testimony, godly living, and acts of mercy and charity to our neighbors constitutes evangelism apart from the proclamation of the Gospel.

I have a personal testimony about the value of personal testimonies. I was led to Christ by a friend who told me about his relationship with Christ. In our conversation he did not present or explain the gospel. In some respects I already knew many elements of the gospel. I was reared in a liberal church under the tutelage of a minister who did not believe in Christ's virgin birth, miracles, or resurrection. Yet in spite of the minister's views, I heard the gospel in Scripture readings, congregational hymns, and choral music. I also heard it from Sunday School teachers, in the catechism, and in part at home. If someone would have asked me before my conversion if God exists or if Christ is God, I would have said yes. I intellectually accepted the truth of the Bible and of much of the gospel. I also knew full well that I was a sinner. I knew virtually nothing about *sola fide.* I thought I was a Christian, but I did not really understand what it means to be a Christian.

When I heard my friend's testimony, I instantly knew that he had something I did not and that I was not a Christian. I still had no formal understanding of *sola fide,* but I suddenly understood that I could not work my way into heaven. When I left my friend after our conversation, I was acutely aware of my sin and my helpless condition. I went immediately to my room. I knelt on the floor by my bed and poured out my soul before God, confessing my sin to him and begging him to pardon and save me. Immediately I experienced an overwhelming sense of forgiveness coupled with a burning affection for Christ. I arose from my knees aware of my salvation. This was the most dramatic turning point of my life. I still did not formally understand *sola fide,* but I had a life-transforming experience of it. I sensed the power of the gospel in my life.

The biblical character to whom I could immediately relate was the publican in Jesus' story of the publican and the Pharisee:

> . . . [Jesus] spoke this parable to some who trusted in themselves that they were righteous, and despised others: "Two men went up to the temple to pray, one a Pharisee and the other a tax collector. The Pharisee stood and prayed thus with himself, 'God, I thank You that I am not like other men—extortioners, unjust, adulterers, or even as this tax collector. I fast twice a week; I give tithes of all that I possess.' And the tax collector, standing afar off, would not so much as raise his eyes to heaven, but beat his breast, saying, 'God, be merciful to me a sinner!' I tell you, this man went down to his house justified rather than the other; for everyone who exalts himself will be abased, and he who humbles himself will be exalted." (Luke 18:9–14)

Prior to my conversion I followed the path of the Pharisee. I was a church member and a tither. I relied on these things to justify myself to God. It is important to see in this parable that the Pharisee thanked God that he was not like other men. He gave lip-service to some measure of grace in his life, yet in the final analysis he trusted in his inherent righteousness. He did not go to his house justified. The tax collector was no theologian. I doubt if he could have articulated the doctrine of *sola fide,* but he lived it in his posture of prayer and went to his house justified.

Many people cannot articulate the fullness of the gospel but nevertheless bear witness of Christ by testifying to what they do understand. Such was the case of the Samaritan woman and the man born blind.

Jesus had a lengthy discourse with the Samaritan woman of Sychar, the woman at the well, telling her about living water, revealing his knowledge of her lurid past, explaining true worship, and revealing to her that he is the Messiah (John 4:5–27). John relates: "The woman then left her waterpot, went her way into the city, and said to the men, 'Come, see a Man who told me all things that I ever did. Could this be the Christ?' Then they went out of the city and came to Him." (John 4:28–30)

The woman did not preach the gospel to the men in the city. All she did was to testify about her encounter with Jesus. She was engaged not in evangelism, but in pre-evangelism. The effect of her testimony was that people took action to learn more about Jesus.

In the case of the man born blind, his condition triggered a discussion between Jesus and his disciples concerning the reason for the man's blindness. Then Jesus healed the man. When his acquaintances asked how his sight had been restored, he simply recounted his meeting with Jesus. Then the man was taken to the Pharisees and interrogated. He declared that Jesus is a prophet (the man did not demonstrate a full awareness of Jesus' identity). This testimony provoked the Pharisees because of their hostility toward Christ. They raised questions about the authenticity of the man's healing. They questioned his parents, who confirmed that he had been born blind and now could see. (John 9:1–23)

The narrative continues: "So they [the Pharisees] again called the man who was blind, and said to him, 'Give God the Glory! We know that this Man is a sinner.' He answered and said, 'Whether He is a sinner or not I do not know. One thing I know: that though I was blind, now I see.'" (John 9:24–25)

The blind man's testimony was limited to the extent of his knowledge. He did not present the gospel to the Jews because he did not yet know the gospel. His understanding of the person of Christ was progressive. Initially he was aware that Jesus was a prophet; the man learned more in another meeting with Jesus. After being cast out for declaring that Jesus is a man from God, the man met Jesus again: "Jesus heard that they had cast him out; and when He had found him, [Jesus] said to him, 'Do you believe in the Son of God?' He answered and said, 'Who is He, Lord, that I may believe in Him?' And Jesus said to him, 'You have both seen

Him and it is He who is talking with you.' Then [the man] said, 'Lord, I believe!' And he worshiped Him." (John 9:35–38)

These episodes make plain the value of personal testimony. But these testimonies, in themselves, did not communicate the gospel.

Our personal testimonies may or may not have relevance to those who hear them. They are partly about Christ, but mostly about ourselves and our experiences. The gospel, on the other hand, has relevance to every person who hears it because it focuses on Christ, on his person and work.

This is in view in the denial of article 18. Though personal testimonies are valid and valuable forms of witness, they fall short of the gospel itself. Our chief task and the task of the church goes beyond the scope of personal testimony to the proclamation, clearly and accurately, of the gospel. Though God may bless our testimonies, it is not they but the gospel that is the power of God unto salvation.

Earlier we mentioned Christ's instructions to his disciples immediately before his ascension: ". . . you shall be witnesses to Me in Jerusalem, and in all Judea and Samaria, and to the end of the earth" (Acts 1:8). John Calvin taught that the church's chief task is to make the invisible kingdom of Christ visible. The church must demonstrate in word and action what the kingdom of Christ is supposed to look like. This takes many forms. For example, James declares that "pure and undefiled religion before God and the Father is this: to visit orphans and widows in their trouble, and to keep oneself unspotted from the world" (James 1:27). This mandate echoes Christ's teaching that we are to feed the hungry, clothe the naked, visit the imprisoned, give shelter and food to the needy. These acts and ministries of mercy all bear witness to Christ and his kingdom, but in themselves they do not proclaim the gospel. Rather they are a living out of the gospel, indicating an obedience to Christ our King.

Civil obedience is another form of witness, one that the early Christian apologists employed to argue for the faith. In a word, how we behave as Christ's disciples in all spheres of life bears witness to him. In the matter of civic behavior, Peter gives the following exhortation: ". . . submit yourselves to every ordinance of man for the Lord's sake, whether to the king as supreme, or to governors, as to those who are sent by him for the punishment of evildoers and for the praise of those who do good. For this is the will of God, that by doing good you may put to silence the ignorance of foolish men—as free, yet not using your liberty as a cloak for vice, but as servants of God. Honor all people. Love the brotherhood. Fear God. Honor the king." (1 Peter 2:13–17)

What is striking about this passage and those that follow (calling servants to be submissive to their masters, wives to be submissive to their husbands, and husbands to give honor to their wives) is that believers are to do all of this "for the Lord's sake."

How does demonstrating proper submissiveness in various spheres do anything for the Lord's sake? I think the answer lies primarily in the nature of all sin as being disobedience to God's authority.

When I disobey God directly, I knowingly defy his authority. When I disobey his delegated authorities, however, I am likewise defying his authority. Conversely, when I obey or submit to even the lowest level of delegated authority, I am thereby submitting to God and his structures of authority. I bear witness to the kingdom of Christ when I obey the authority structures God has ordered for that kingdom.

There are other ways in which we bear witness to Christ. One is through apologetics, presenting the case for the truth claims of Christianity and defending the faith against its stated enemies. Yet we can and must distinguish between apologetics and evangelism, just as we distinguish between *kērygma* and *didachē*.

Our personal behavior is also a form of witness to Christ. We are called to imitate Christ as Christ imitates God. Luther said that every Christian is called to be Christ to his neighbor. Luther did not mean that we can actually be Christ or that we can save our neighbors. Luther meant that we are to be Christ's ambassadors or representatives to our neighbors, so that we communicate Christ to them by our actions. Paul deplored the situation when believers present the wrong example and Gentiles blaspheme because of them. Peter said: "Beloved, I beg you as sojourners and pilgrims, abstain from fleshly lusts which war against the soul, having your conduct honorable among the Gentiles, that when they speak against you as evildoers, they may, by your good works which they observe, glorify God in the day of visitation" (1 Peter 2:11–12).

We are to bear witness to Christ by honorable conduct. We are to be people whose word can be trusted, whose yes means yes and whose no means no. We are to be salt and light in a dying world.

All these things involve witness to Christ, but they are not evangelism. The term *martyr* comes into the English language from the Greek *martyria,* "to witness." Not all martyrs are witnesses to Christ, but in terms of our language, not all witnesses are martyrs.

In popular Christian nomenclature the term *witnessing* is often used as a synonym for *evangelism.* This reflects some confusion with the terms. The two are not identical, but are related as genus and species. Witnessing is the generic term, while evangelism is a specific form. Evangelism is a particular form of witnessing. It is the proclamation of the content of the gospel. All evangelism is witness; but not all witness is evangelism. Article 18 denies that all forms of witnessing, such as godly living, explicitly declare the content of the gospel.

Evangelicals United

> As evangelicals united in the Gospel, we promise to watch over and care for one another, to pray for and forgive one another, and to reach out in love and truth to God's people everywhere, for we are one family, one in the Holy Spirit, and one in Christ.
>
> Centuries ago it was truly said that in things necessary there must be unity, in things less than necessary there must be liberty, and in all things there must be charity. We see all these Gospel truths as necessary.
>
> Now to God, the Author of the truth and grace of this Gospel, through Jesus Christ, its subject and our Lord, be praise and glory for ever and ever. Amen.

Because Christ has never rescinded the Great Commission, we as his disciples are under the urgent necessity to bring the wonderful good news of the gospel to every man and woman, boy and girl, throughout the world.

We pray that the Lord through his mercy and grace will see fit to bless the reaffirmations and commitments about the gospel made in *The Gospel of Jesus Christ.*

The concluding statement puts the affirmations and denials in proper perspective. They are the foundation that expresses the mission of the church. For the church to be faithful to the Great Commission, we must get the gospel right. When we do, we will both energize the church's activity and encourage deep and abiding unity among Evangelicals.

Appendix 1

The Gift of Salvation

> "For God so loved the world that he gave his only Son, that whoever believes in him should not perish but have eternal life. For God sent the Son into the world, not to condemn the world, but that the world might be saved through him." (John 3:16–17)

[1] We give thanks to God that in recent years many Evangelicals and Catholics, ourselves among them, have been able to express a common faith in Christ and so to acknowledge one another as brothers and sisters in Christ. We confess together one God, the Father, the Son[1] and the Holy Spirit; we confess Jesus Christ the Incarnate Son of God; we affirm the binding authority of Holy Scripture, God's inspired Word; and we acknowledge the Apostles' and Nicene creeds as faithful witnesses to that Word.

[2] The effectiveness of our witness for Christ depends upon the work of the Holy Spirit, who calls and empowers us to confess together the meaning of the salvation promised and accomplished in Christ Jesus our Lord. Through prayer and study of Holy Scripture, and aided by the Church's reflection on the sacred text from earliest times, we have found that, notwithstanding some persistent and serious differences, we can together bear witness to the gift of salvation in Jesus Christ. To this saving gift we now testify, speaking not for, but from and to, our several communities.

[3] God created us to manifest his glory and to give us eternal life in fellowship with himself, but our disobedience intervened and brought

us under condemnation. As members of the fallen human race, we come into the world estranged from God and in a state of rebellion. This original sin is compounded by our personal acts of sinfulness. The catastrophic consequences of sin are such that we are powerless to restore the ruptured bonds of union with God. Only in the light of what God has done to restore our fellowship with him do we see the full enormity of our loss. The gravity of our plight and the greatness of God's love are brought home to us by the life, suffering, death, and resurrection of Jesus Christ. "God so loved the world that he gave his only Son, that whoever believes in him should not perish but have eternal life" (John 3:16).

[4] God the Creator is also God the Redeemer, offering salvation to the world. "God desires all to be saved and come to a knowledge[2] of the truth" (1 Timothy 2:4). The restoration of communion with God is absolutely dependent upon Jesus Christ, true God and true man, for he is "the one mediator between God and men" (1 Timothy 2:5), and "there is no other name under heaven given among men by which we must be saved" (Acts 4:12). Jesus said, "No one comes to the Father but by me" (John 14:6). He is the holy and righteous one who was put to death for our sins, "the righteous for the unrighteous, that he might bring us to God" (1 Peter 3:18).

[5] The New Testament speaks of salvation in various ways. Salvation is ultimate or eschatological rescue from sin and its consequences, the final state of safety and glory to which we are brought in both body and soul. "Since, therefore, we are now justified by his blood, much more shall we be saved by him from the wrath of God." "Salvation is nearer to us now than when we first believed" (Romans 5:9;[3] 13:11). Salvation is also a present reality. We are told that "he saved us, not because of deeds done by us in righteousness, but in virtue of his own mercy" (Titus 3:5). The present reality of salvation is an anticipation and foretaste of salvation in its promised fullness.

[6] Always it is clear that the work of redemption has been accomplished by Christ's atoning sacrifice on the cross. "Christ redeemed us from the curse of the law by becoming a curse for us" (Galatians 3:13). Scripture describes the consequences of Christ's redemptive work in several ways, among which are: justification, reconciliation, restoration of friendship with God, and rebirth from above by which we are adopted as children of God and made heirs of the Kingdom. "When the time had fully come, God sent his son, born of a woman, born under law, that we might receive the adoption of sons" (Galatians 4:4–5).

[7] Justification is central to the scriptural account of salvation, and its meaning has been much debated between Protestants and Catholics.

We agree that justification is not earned by any good works or merits of our own; it is entirely God's gift, conferred through the Father's sheer graciousness, out of the love that he bears us in his Son, who suffered on our behalf and rose from the dead for our justification. Jesus was "put to death for our trespasses and raised for our justification" (Romans 4:25). In justification, God, on the basis of Christ's righteousness alone, declares us to be no longer his rebellious enemies but his forgiven friends, and by virtue of his declaration it is so.

[8] The New Testament makes it clear that the gift of justification is received through faith. "By grace you have been saved through faith; and this is not your own doing, it is the gift of God" (Ephesians 2:8). By faith, which is also the gift of God, we repent of our sins and freely adhere to the gospel,[4] the good news of God's saving work for us in Christ. By our response of faith to Christ, we enter into the blessings promised by the gospel. Faith is not merely intellectual assent but an act of the whole person, involving the mind, the will, and the affections, issuing in a changed life. We understand that what we here affirm is in agreement with what the Reformation traditions have meant by justification by faith alone *(sola fide).*

[9] In justification we receive the gift of the Holy Spirit, through whom the love of God is poured forth into our hearts (Romans 5:5). The grace of Christ and the gift of the Spirit received through faith (Galatians 3:14) are experienced and expressed in diverse ways by different Christians and in different Christian traditions, but God's gift is never dependent upon our human experience or our ways of expressing that experience.

[10] While faith is inherently personal, it is not a purely private possession but involves participation in the body of Christ. By baptism we are visibly incorporated into the community of faith and committed to a life of discipleship. "We were buried therefore with him by baptism into death, so that as Christ was raised from the dead by the glory of the Father, we too might walk in newness of life" (Romans 6:4).

[11] By their faith and baptism, Christians are bound to live according to the law of love in obedience to Jesus Christ the Lord. Scripture calls this the life of holiness, of sanctification. "Since we have these promises, dear friends, let us purify ourselves from everything that contaminates body and spirit, perfecting holiness out of reverence for God" (2 Corinthians 7:1). Sanctification is not fully accomplished at the beginning of our life in Christ, but is progressively furthered as we struggle, with God's grace and help, against adversity and temptation. In this struggle we are assured that Christ's grace will be sufficient for us, enabling us to persevere to the end. When we fail, we can still turn

to God in humble repentance and confidently ask for, and receive, his forgiveness.

[12] We may therefore have assured hope for the eternal life promised to us in Christ. As we have shared in his sufferings, we will share in his final glory. "We shall be like him, for we shall see him as he is" (1 John 3:2). While we dare not presume upon the grace of God, the promise of God in Christ is utterly reliable, and faith in that promise overcomes anxiety about our eternal future. We are bound by faith itself to have firm hope, to encourage one another in that hope, and in such hope we rejoice. For believers "through faith are shielded by God's power until the coming of the salvation to be revealed in the last time" (1 Peter 1:5).

[13] Thus it is that as justified sinners we have been saved, we are being saved, and we will be saved. All this is the gift of God. Faith issues in a confident hope for a new heaven and a new earth in which God's creating and redeeming purposes are gloriously fulfilled. "Therefore God has highly exalted him and bestowed on him the name which is above every name, that at the name of Jesus every knee should bow, in heaven and on earth and under the earth, and every tongue confess that Jesus Christ is Lord, to the glory of God the Father" (Philippians 2:9–11).

[14] As believers we are sent into the world and commissioned to be bearers of the good news, to serve one another in love, to do good to all, and to evangelize everyone everywhere. It is our responsibility and firm resolve to bring to the whole world the tidings of God's love and of the salvation accomplished in our crucified, risen, and returning Lord. Many are in grave peril of being eternally lost because they do not know the way to salvation.

[15] In obedience to the Great Commission of our Lord, we commit ourselves to evangelizing everyone. We must share the fullness of God's saving truth with all, including members of our several communities. Evangelicals must speak the gospel to Catholics and Catholics to Evangelicals, always speaking the truth in love, so that "working hard to maintain the unity of the Spirit in the bond of peace . . . the body of Christ may be built up until we all reach unity in the faith and in the knowledge of the Son of God" (Ephesians 4:3, 12–13).

[16] Moreover, we defend religious freedom for all. Such freedom is grounded in the dignity of the human person created in the image of God[5] and must be protected also in civil law.

[17] We must not allow our witness as Christians to be compromised by half-hearted[6] discipleship or needlessly divisive disputes. While we rejoice in the unity we have discovered and are confident of the fun-

damental truths about the gift of salvation we have affirmed, we recognize that there are necessarily interrelated questions that require further and urgent exploration. Among such questions are these: the meaning of baptismal regeneration, the Eucharist, and sacramental grace; the historic uses of the language of justification as it relates to imputed and transformative righteousness; the normative status of justification in relation to all Christian doctrine; the assertion that while justification is by faith alone, the faith that receives salvation is never alone; diverse understandings of merit, reward, purgatory, and indulgences; Marian devotion and the assistance of the saints in the life of salvation; and the possibility of salvation for those who have not been evangelized.

[18] On these and other questions, we recognize that there are also some differences within both the Evangelical and Catholic communities. We are committed to examining these questions further in our continuing conversations. All who truly believe in Jesus Christ are brothers and sisters in the Lord and must not allow their differences, however important, to undermine this great truth, or to deflect them from bearing witness together to God's gift of salvation in Christ. "I appeal to you, brothers, in the name of our Lord Jesus Christ, that all of you agree with one another so that there may be no divisions among you and that you may be perfectly united in mind and thought" (1 Corinthians 1:10).

[19] As Evangelicals who thank God for the heritage of the Reformation and affirm with conviction its classic confessions, as Catholics who are conscientiously faithful to the teaching of the Catholic Church, and as disciples together of the Lord Jesus Christ who recognize our debt to our Christian forebears and our obligations to our contemporaries and those who will come after us, we affirm our unity in the gospel that we have here professed. In our continuing discussions, we seek no unity other than unity in the truth. Only unity in the truth can be pleasing to the Lord and Savior whom we together serve, for he is "the way, the truth, and the life" (John 14:6).

Evangelicals[7]

Dr. Gerald L. Bray (Beeson Divinity School)
Dr. Bill Bright (Campus Crusade for Christ)
Dr. Harold O. J. Brown (Trinity Evangelical Divinity School)
Mr. Charles Colson (Prison Fellowship)

Bishop William C. Frey (Episcopal Church)
Dr. Timothy George (Beeson Divinity School)
Dr. Os Guinness (The Trinity Forum)
Dr. Kent R. Hill (Eastern Nazarene College)
The Rev.[8] Max Lucado (Oak Hills Church of Christ, San Antonio, Texas)
Dr. T. M. Moore (Chesapeake Theological Seminary)
Dr. Richard Mouw (Fuller Theological Seminary)
Dr. Mark A. Noll (Wheaton College)
Mr. Brian F. O'Connell (Interdev)
Dr. Thomas Oden (Drew University)
Dr. James I. Packer[9] (Regent College, British Columbia)
Dr. Timothy R. Phillips (Wheaton College)
Dr. John Rodgers (Trinity Episcopal School for Ministry)
Dr. John Woodbridge (Trinity Evangelical Divinity School)[10]

Roman Catholics

Fr.[11] James J. Buckley (Loyola College in Maryland)
Fr. J. A. Di Noia, O.P. (Dominican House of Studies)
Fr. Avery Dulles, S.J. (Fordham University)
Fr. Thomas Guarino (Seton Hall University)
Dr. Peter Kreeft (Boston College)
Fr. Matthew L. Lamb (Boston College)
Fr. Eugene LaVerdiere, S.S.S. (Emmanuel[12])
Fr. Francis Martin (John Paul II Institute for Studies on Marriage and Family)
Mr. Ralph Martin (Renewal Ministries)
Fr. Richard John Neuhaus (Religion and Public Life)
Mr. Michael Novak (American Enterprise Institute)
Fr. Edward Oakes, S.J. (Regis University)
Fr. Thomas P. Rausch, S.J. (Loyola Marymount University)
Mr. George Weigel (Ethics and Public Policy Center)
Dr. Robert Louis Wilken (University of Virginia)[13]

Appendix 2

The Gospel of Jesus Christ: An Evangelical Celebration

"For God so loved the world that he gave his one and only Son, that whoever believes in him shall not perish but have eternal life" (John 3:16).

"Sing to the Lord, for he has done glorious things; let this be known to all the world" (Isaiah 12:5).

Preamble

The Gospel of Jesus Christ is news, good news: the best and most important news that any human being ever hears.

This Gospel declares the only way to know God in peace, love, and joy is through the reconciling death of Jesus Christ the risen Lord.

This Gospel is the central message of the Holy Scriptures, and is the true key to understanding them.

This Gospel identifies Jesus Christ, the Messiah of Israel, as the Son of God and God the Son, the second Person of the Holy Trinity, whose incarnation, ministry, death, resurrection, and ascension fulfilled the Father's saving will. His death for sins and his resurrection from the dead were promised beforehand by the prophets and attested by eyewitnesses. In God's own time and in God's own way, Jesus Christ shall return as glorious Lord and Judge of all (1 Thess. 4:13–18; Matt. 25:31–32). He is now giving the Holy Spirit from the Father to all those who are truly his. The three Persons of the Trinity thus combine in the work of saving sinners.

This Gospel sets forth Jesus Christ as the living Savior, Master, Life, and Hope of all who put their trust in him. It tells us that the eternal destiny of all people depends on whether they are savingly related to Jesus Christ.

This Gospel is the only Gospel: there is no other; and to change its substance is to pervert and indeed destroy it. This Gospel is so simple that small children can understand it, and it is so profound that studies by the wisest theologians will never exhaust its riches.

All Christians are called to unity in love and unity in truth. As evangelicals who derive our very name from the Gospel, we celebrate this great good news of God's saving work in Jesus Christ as the true bond of Christian unity, whether among organized churches and denominations or in the many transdenominational cooperative enterprises of Christians together.

The Bible declares that all who truly trust in Christ and his Gospel are sons and daughters of God through grace, and hence are our brothers and sisters in Christ.

All who are justified experience reconciliation with the Father, full remission of sins, transition from the kingdom of darkness to the kingdom of light, the reality of being a new creature in Christ, and the fellowship of the Holy Spirit. They enjoy access to the Father with all the peace and joy that this brings.

The Gospel requires of all believers worship, which means constant praise and giving of thanks to God, submission to all that he has revealed in his written word, prayerful dependence on him, and vigilance lest his truth be even inadvertently compromised or obscured.

To share the joy and hope of this Gospel is a supreme privilege. It is also an abiding obligation, for the Great Commission of Jesus Christ still stands: proclaim the Gospel everywhere, he said, teaching, baptizing, and making disciples.

By embracing the following declaration we affirm our commitment to this task, and with it our allegiance to Christ himself, to the Gospel itself, and to each other as fellow evangelical believers.

The Gospel

This Gospel of Jesus Christ which God sets forth in the infallible Scriptures combines Jesus' own declaration of the present reality of the kingdom of God with the apostles' account of the person, place, and work of Christ, and how sinful humans benefit from it. The Patristic Rule of Faith, the historic creeds, the Reformation confessions, and the doctrinal bases of later evangelical bodies all witness to the substance of this biblical message.

The heart of the Gospel is that our holy, loving Creator, confronted with human hostility and rebellion, has chosen in his own freedom and faithfulness to become our holy, loving Redeemer and Restorer. The Father has sent the Son to be the Savior of the world (1 John 4:14): it is through his one and only Son that God's one and only plan of salvation is implemented. So Peter announced: "Salvation is found in no one else, for there is no other name under heaven given to men by which we must be saved" (Acts 4:12). And Christ himself taught: "I am the way, the truth and the life. No one comes to the Father except through me" (John 14:6).

Through the Gospel we learn that we human beings, who were made for fellowship with God, are by nature—that is, "in Adam" (1 Cor. 15:22)—dead in sin, unresponsive to and separated from our Maker. We are constantly twisting his truth, breaking his law, belittling his goals and standards, and offending his holiness by our unholiness, so that we truly are "without hope and without God in the world" (Rom. 1:18–32, 3:9–20; Eph. 2:1–3, 12). Yet God in grace took the initiative to reconcile us to himself through the sinless life and vicarious death of his beloved Son (Eph. 2:4–10; Rom. 3:21–24).

The Father sent the Son to free us from the dominion of sin and Satan, and to make us God's children and friends. Jesus paid our penalty in our place on his cross, satisfying the retributive demands of divine justice by shedding his blood in sacrifice and so making possible justification for all who trust in him (Rom. 3:25–26). The Bible describes this mighty substitutionary transaction as the achieving of ransom, reconciliation, redemption, propitiation, and conquest of evil powers (Matt. 20:28; 2 Cor. 5:18–21; Rom. 3:23–25; John 12:31; Col. 2:15). It secures for us a restored relationship with God that brings pardon and peace, acceptance and access, and adoption into God's family (Col. 1:20, 2:13–14; Rom. 5:1–2; Gal. 4:4–7; 1 Pet. 3:18). The faith in God and in Christ to which the Gospel calls us is a trustful outgoing of our hearts to lay hold of these promised and proffered benefits.

This Gospel further proclaims the bodily resurrection, ascension, and enthronement of Jesus as evidence of the efficacy of his once-for-all sacrifice for us, of the reality of his present personal ministry to us, and of the certainty of his future return to glorify us (1 Cor. 15; Heb. 1:1–4, 2:1–18, 4:14–16, 7:1–10:25). In the life of faith as the Gospel presents it, believers are united with their risen Lord, communing with him, and looking to him in repentance and hope for empowering through the Holy Spirit, so that henceforth they may not sin but serve him truly.

God's justification of those who trust him, according to the Gospel, is a decisive transition, here and now, from a state of condemnation and wrath because of their sins to one of acceptance and favor by virtue of Jesus' flawless obedience culminating in his voluntary sin-bearing death. God "justifies the wicked" (ungodly: Rom. 4:5) by imputing (reckoning, crediting, counting, accounting) righteousness to them and ceasing to count their sins against them (Rom. 4:1–8). Sinners receive through faith in Christ alone "the gift of righteousness" (Rom. 1:17, 5:17; Phil. 3:9) and thus become "the righteousness of God" in him who was "made sin" for them (2 Cor. 5:21).

As our sins were reckoned to Christ, so Christ's righteousness is reckoned to us. This is justification by the imputation of Christ's righteousness. All we bring to the transaction is our need of it. Our faith in the God who bestows it, the Father, the Son, and the Holy Spirit, is itself the fruit of God's grace. Faith links us savingly to Jesus, but inasmuch as it involves an acknowledgment that we have no merit of our own, it is confessedly not a meritorious work.

The Gospel assures us that all who have entrusted their lives to Jesus Christ are born-again children of God (John 1:12), indwelt, empowered, and assured of their status and hope by the Holy Spirit (Rom. 7:6, 8:9–17). The moment we truly believe in Christ, the Father declares us righteous in him and begins conforming us to his likeness. Genuine faith acknowledges and depends upon Jesus as Lord and shows itself in growing obedience to the divine commands, though this contributes nothing to the ground of our justification (James 2:14–26; Heb. 6:1–12).

By his sanctifying grace, Christ works within us through faith, renewing our fallen nature and leading us to real maturity, that measure of development which is meant by "the fullness of Christ" (Eph. 4:13). The Gospel calls us to live as obedient servants of Christ and as his emissaries in the world, doing justice, loving mercy, and helping all in need, thus seeking to bear witness to the kingdom of Christ. At death, Christ takes the believer to himself (Phil. 1:21) for unimaginable joy in the ceaseless worship of God (Rev. 22:1–5).

Salvation in its full sense is from the guilt of sin in the past, the power of sin in the present, and the presence of sin in the future. Thus, while in foretaste believers enjoy salvation now, they still await its fullness (Mark 14:61–62; Heb. 9:28). Salvation is a Trinitarian reality, initiated by the Father, implemented by the Son, and applied by the Holy Spirit. It has a global dimension, for God's plan is to save believers out of every tribe and tongue (Rev. 5:9) to be his church, a new humanity, the people of God, the body and bride of Christ, and the community of the Holy Spirit. All the heirs of final salvation are called here and now to serve their Lord and each other in love, to share in the fellowship of Jesus' sufferings, and to work together to make Christ known to the whole world.

We learn from the Gospel that, as all have sinned, so all who do not receive Christ will be judged according to their just deserts as measured by God's holy law, and face eternal retributive punishment.

Unity in the Gospel

Christians are commanded to love each other despite differences of race, gender, privilege, and social, political, and economic background (John 13:34–35; Gal. 3:28–29), and to be of one mind wherever possible (John 17:20–21; Phil. 2:2; Rom. 14:1–15:13). We know that divisions among Christians hinder our witness in the world, and we desire greater mutual understanding and truth-speaking in love. We know too that as trustees of God's revealed truth we cannot embrace any form of doctrinal indifferentism, or relativism, or pluralism by which God's truth is sacrificed for a false peace.

Doctrinal disagreements call for debate. Dialogue for mutual understanding and, if possible, narrowing of the differences is valuable, doubly so when the avowed goal is unity in primary things, with liberty in secondary things, and charity in all things.

In the foregoing paragraphs, an attempt has been made to state what is primary and essential in the Gospel as evangelicals understand it. Useful dialogue, however, requires not only charity in our attitudes, but also clarity in our utterances. Our extended analysis of justification by faith alone through Christ alone reflects our belief that Gospel truth is of crucial importance and is not always well understood and correctly affirmed. For added clarity, out of love for God's truth and Christ's church, we now cast the key points of what has been said into specific affirmations and denials regarding the Gospel and our unity in it and in Christ.

Affirmations and Denials

1. We affirm that the Gospel entrusted to the church is, in the first instance, God's Gospel (Mark 1:14; Rom. 1:1). God is its author,

and he reveals it to us in and by his Word. Its authority and truth rest on him alone. □ We deny that the truth or authority of the Gospel derives from any human insight or invention (Gal. 1:1–11). We also deny that the truth or authority of the Gospel rests on the authority of any particular church or human institution.

2. We affirm that the Gospel is the saving power of God in that the Gospel effects salvation to everyone who believes, without distinction (Rom. 1:16). This efficacy of the Gospel is by the power of God himself (1 Cor. 1:18). □ We deny that the power of the Gospel rests in the eloquence of the preacher, the technique of the evangelist, or the persuasion of rational argument (1 Cor. 1:21; 2:1–5).
3. We affirm that the Gospel diagnoses the universal human condition as one of sinful rebellion against God, which, if unchanged, will lead each person to eternal loss under God's condemnation. □ We deny any rejection of the fallenness of human nature or any assertion of the natural goodness, or divinity, of the human race.
4. We affirm that Jesus Christ is the only way of salvation, the only mediator between God and humanity (John 14:6; 1 Tim. 2:5). □ We deny that anyone is saved in any other way than by Jesus Christ and his Gospel. The Bible offers no hope that sincere worshipers of other religions will be saved without personal faith in Jesus Christ.
5. We affirm that the church is commanded by God and is therefore under divine obligation to preach the Gospel to every living person (Luke 24:47; Matt. 28:18–19). □ We deny that any particular class or group of persons, whatever their ethnic or cultural identity, may be ignored or passed over in the preaching of the Gospel (1 Cor. 9:19–22). God purposes a global church made up from people of every tribe, language, and nation (Rev. 7:9).
6. We affirm that faith in Jesus Christ as the divine Word (or Logos, John 1:1), the second Person of the Trinity, co-eternal and co-essential with the Father and the Holy Spirit (Heb. 1:3), is foundational to faith in the Gospel. □ We deny that any view of Jesus Christ which reduces or rejects his full deity is Gospel faith or will avail to salvation.
7. We affirm that Jesus Christ is God incarnate (John 1:14). The virgin-born descendant of David (Rom. 1:3), he had a true human nature, was subject to the Law of God (Gal. 4:5), and was like us at all points, except without sin (Heb. 2:17, 7:26–28). We affirm that faith in the true humanity of Christ is essential to faith in the

Gospel. ☐ We deny that anyone who rejects the humanity of Christ, his incarnation, or his sinlessness, or who maintains that these truths are not essential to the Gospel, will be saved (1 John 4:2–3).

8. We affirm that the atonement of Christ by which, in his obedience, he offered a perfect sacrifice, propitiating the Father by paying for our sins and satisfying divine justice on our behalf according to God's eternal plan, is an essential element of the Gospel. ☐ We deny that any view of the Atonement that rejects the substitutionary satisfaction of divine justice, accomplished vicariously for believers, is compatible with the teaching of the Gospel.
9. We affirm that Christ's saving work included both his life and his death on our behalf (Gal. 3:13). We declare that faith in the perfect obedience of Christ by which he fulfilled all the demands of the Law of God in our behalf is essential to the Gospel. ☐ We deny that our salvation was achieved merely or exclusively by the death of Christ without reference to his life of perfect righteousness.
10. We affirm that the bodily resurrection of Christ from the dead is essential to the biblical Gospel (1 Cor. 15:14). ☐ We deny the validity of any so-called gospel that denies the historical reality of the bodily resurrection of Christ.
11. We affirm that the biblical doctrine of justification by faith alone in Christ alone is essential to the Gospel (Rom. 3:28; 4:5; Gal. 2:16). ☐ We deny that any person can believe the biblical Gospel and at the same time reject the apostolic teaching of justification by faith alone in Christ alone. We also deny that there is more than one true Gospel (Gal. 1:6–9).
12. We affirm that the doctrine of the imputation (reckoning or counting) both of our sins to Christ and of his righteousness to us, whereby our sins are fully forgiven and we are fully accepted, is essential to the biblical Gospel (2 Cor. 5:19–21). ☐ We deny that we are justified by the righteousness of Christ infused into us or by any righteousness that is thought to inhere within us.
13. We affirm that the righteousness of Christ by which we are justified is properly his own, which he achieved apart from us, in and by his perfect obedience. This righteousness is counted, reckoned, or imputed to us by the forensic (that is, legal) declaration of God, as the sole ground of our justification. ☐ We deny that any works we perform at any stage of our existence add to the merit of Christ or earn for us any merit that contributes in any way to the ground of our justification (Gal. 2:16; Eph. 2:8–9; Titus 3:5).

14. We affirm that, while all believers are indwelt by the Holy Spirit and are in the process of being made holy and conformed to the image of Christ, those consequences of justification are not its ground. God declares us just, remits our sins, and adopts us as his children, by his grace alone, and through faith alone, because of Christ alone, while we are still sinners (Rom. 4:5). □ We deny that believers must be inherently righteous by virtue of their cooperation with God's life-transforming grace before God will declare them justified in Christ. We are justified while we are still sinners.
15. We affirm that saving faith results in sanctification, the transformation of life in growing conformity to Christ through the power of the Holy Spirit. Sanctification means ongoing repentance, a life of turning from sin to serve Jesus Christ in grateful reliance on him as one's Lord and Master (Gal. 5:22–25; Rom. 8:4, 13–14). □ We reject any view of justification which divorces it from our sanctifying union with Christ and our increasing conformity to his image through prayer, repentance, cross-bearing, and life in the Spirit.
16. We affirm that saving faith includes mental assent to the content of the Gospel, acknowledgment of our own sin and need, and personal trust and reliance upon Christ and his work. □ We deny that saving faith includes only mental acceptance of the Gospel, and that justification is secured by a mere outward profession of faith. We further deny that any element of saving faith is a meritorious work or earns salvation for us.
17. We affirm that, although true doctrine is vital for spiritual health and well-being, we are not saved by doctrine. Doctrine is necessary to inform us how we may be saved by Christ, but it is Christ who saves. □ We deny that the doctrines of the Gospel can be rejected without harm. Denial of the Gospel brings spiritual ruin and exposes us to God's judgment.
18. We affirm that Jesus Christ commands his followers to proclaim the Gospel to all living persons, evangelizing everyone everywhere, and discipling believers within the fellowship of the church. A full and faithful witness to Christ includes the witness of personal testimony, godly living, and acts of mercy and charity to our neighbor, without which the preaching of the Gospel appears barren. □ We deny that the witness of personal testimony, godly living, and acts of mercy and charity to our neighbors constitute evangelism apart from the proclamation of the Gospel.

Our Commitment

As evangelicals united in the Gospel, we promise to watch over and care for one another, to pray for and forgive one another, and to reach out in love and truth to God's people everywhere, for we are one family, one in the Holy Spirit, and one in Christ.

Centuries ago it was truly said that in things necessary there must be unity, in things less than necessary there must be liberty, and in all things there must be charity. We see all these Gospel truths as necessary.

Now to God, the Author of the truth and grace of this Gospel, through Jesus Christ, its subject and our Lord, be praise and glory for ever and ever. Amen.

The Drafting Committee

John N. Akers
John Ankerberg
John Armstrong
D. A. Carson
Keith Davy
Maxie Dunnam
Timothy George
Scott Hafemann
Erwin Lutzer
Harold Myra
David Neff
Thomas Oden
J. I. Packer
R. C. Sproul
John Woodbridge

Confirmed Endorsing Committee[1]

Eric Alexander
C. Fitzsimmons Allison
Bill Anderson
J. Kerby Anderson
Don Argue
Kay Arthur
Myron S. Augsburger
Theodore Baehr
Joel Belz
Henri Blocher
Donald G. Bloesch
Scott Bolinder
John Bolt
Gerald Bray
Bill Bright
Harold O. J. Brown
Stephen Brown
George Brushaber
David Cerullo
Peter Cha
Daniel R. Chamberlain
Bryan Chapell

David K. Clark
Edmund Clowney
Robert Coleman
Chuck Colson
Clyde Cook
Lane T. Dennis
David S. Dockery
Stuart Epperson
James Erickson
Tony Evans
Jerry Falwell
Sinclair Ferguson
Dwight Gibson
Wayne Grudem
Stan N. Gundry
Brandt Gustavson
Corkie Haan
Mimi Haddad
Ben Haden
B. Sam Hart
Bob Hawkins, Jr.
Wendell Hawley
Jack W. Hayford
Stephen A. Hayner
Jim Henry
Roberta Hestenes
Oswald Hoffman
R. Kent Hughes
Bill Hybels
Kay Cole James
David Jeremiah
Arthur P. Johnston
Howard Jones
Walter C. Kaiser, Jr.
Kenneth Kantzer
D. James Kennedy
Jay Kesler
In Ho Koh
Woodrow Kroll
Beverly LaHaye
Tim LaHaye
Richard Land
Richard G. Lee
Duane Litfin
Crawford Loritts
Max Lucado
John MacArthur
Marlin Maddoux
Bill McCartney
David Melvin
Jesse Miranda
Beth Moore
Peter C. Moore
T. M. Moore
Richard J. Mouw
Thomas J. Nettles
Roger Nicole
Luis Palau
Earl R. Palmer
Hee Min Park
Phillip Porter
Paul Pressler
Ray Pritchard
Robert Ricker
Pat Robertson
John Rodgers
Adrian Rogers
Doug Ross
Joseph F. Ryan
John Scott
David Short
Ronald J. Sider
Russell Spittler
James J. Stamoolis
Charles F. Stanley
Brian Stiller
John Stott
Joseph Stowell
Stephen Strang
Charles Swindoll
Joni Eareckson Tada
Thomas E. Trask

Augustin B. Vencer, Jr.
Paul L. Walker
John F. Walvoord
Raleigh Washington
Greg Waybright
David F. Wells
Luder Whitlock
Bruce H. Wilkinson
David K. Winter
Ravi Zacharias

Notes

Preface

1. *Evangelicals and Catholics Together: The Christian Mission in the Third Millennium* (1994). Printed in *First Things,* no. 43 (May 1994): 15–22.
2. *The Gift of Salvation* (1997). Printed in *Christianity Today,* 8 December 1997, pp. 35–36; 38; and *First Things,* no. 79 (January 1998): 20–23.
3. *The Gospel of Jesus Christ: An Evangelical Celebration* (1999). Printed in *Christianity Today,* 14 June 1999, pp. 51–56.

Chapter 1, Unity and the Gospel

1. *Canons and Decrees of the Council of Trent: Original Text with English Translation,* trans. H. J. Schroeder (London: Herder, 1941), pp. 29–46.
2. *The Gift of Salvation* (1997). Printed in *Christianity Today,* 8 December 1997, pp. 35–36; 38; and *First Things,* no. 79 (January 1998): 20–23.
3. R. C. Sproul, *Faith Alone: The Evangelical Doctrine of Justification* (Grand Rapids: Baker, 1995), pp. 75–90.

Chapter 2, Evangelicals and the Evangel

1. *Evangelicals and Catholics Together: The Christian Mission in the Third Millennium* (1994). Printed in *First Things,* no. 43 (May 1994): 15–22.
2. R. C. Sproul, *Faith Alone: The Evangelical Doctrine of Justification* (Grand Rapids: Baker, 1995), pp. 117–31.
3. *Catechism of the Catholic Church* (Liguori, Mo.: Liguori, 1994).
4. *The Gift of Salvation* (1997). Printed in *Christianity Today,* 8 December 1997, pp. 35–36, 38; and *First Things,* no. 79 (January 1998): 20–23.
5. *The Gospel of Jesus Christ: An Evangelical Celebration* (1999). Printed in *Christianity Today,* 14 June 1999, pp. 51–56.

Chapter 3, Our Need for Justification

1. *The Gift of Salvation* (1997). Printed in *Christianity Today,* 8 December 1997, pp. 35–36, 38; and *First Things,* no. 79 (January 1998): 20–23.

2. *Evangelicals and Catholics Together: The Christian Mission in the Third Millennium* (1994). Printed in *First Things,* no. 43 (May 1994): 15–22.

3. Alliance of Confessing Evangelicals, *An Open Letter of Pastoral Concern* (Philadelphia: Alliance of Confessing Evangelicals, 1998). A copy of this letter may be obtained from ACE's web site (http://www.remembrancer/ace) or from its offices (P.O. Box 2000, Philadelphia, PA 19103).

4. Alliance of Confessing Evangelicals, *Justification by Faith Alone* (Philadelphia: Alliance of Confessing Evangelicals, 1998). A copy of this statement may be obtained from ACE's web site or offices (see n. 3 for addresses).

5. Randy Frame, "Evangelicals, Catholics Issue Salvation Accord," *Christianity Today,* 12 January 1998, p. 62.

6. Timothy George, Thomas C. Oden, and J. I. Packer, "An Open Letter about *The Gift of Salvation,*" *Christianity Today,* 27 April 1998, p. 9.

Chapter 4, The Basis of Our Justification

1. *Canons and Decrees of the Council of Trent: Original Text with English Translation,* trans. H. J. Schroeder (London: Herder, 1941), p. 52. This is canon 8 of "Canons on the Sacraments in General" from the seventh session.

2. Ibid., p. 35. Chapter 9 of the sixth session.

3. Ibid., p. 38. Chapter 12 of the sixth session.

Chapter 5, Divisive Disputes and Legitimate Questions

1. Timothy George, Thomas C. Oden, and J. I. Packer, "An Open Letter about *The Gift of Salvation,*" *Christianity Today,* 27 April 1998, p. 9.

2. *Canons and Decrees of the Council of Trent: Original Text with English Translation,* trans. H. J. Schroeder (London: Herder, 1941), p. 79., "Canons on the Most Holy Sacrament of the Eucharist," thirteenth session.

3. Ibid., p. 149., "Canons on the Sacrifice of the Mass," canon 1, twenty-second session.

4. Pope Paul VI, *Mysterium fidei* (1965). An English translation of this encyclical is perhaps most accessible on the Vatican's web site (http://www.vatican.va).

5. J. I. Packer, "Introductory Essay," in James Buchanan, *The Doctrine of Justification: An Outline of Its History in the Church and of Its Exposition from Scripture* (London: Banner of Truth, 1961), pp. viii–ix.

6. Albrecht Beutel, Karin Bornkamm, Gerhard Ebeling, Reinhard Schwarz, and Johannes Wallmann, "No Consensus on the *Joint Declaration on the Doctrine of Justification:* A Critical Evaluation by Professors of Protestant Theology," trans. Oliver K. Olson, *Lutheran Quarterly* 12 (Summer 1998): 194. This statement appeared originally in the *Frankfurter Allgemeine Zeitung,* 29 January 1998.

7. Edward E. Plowman, "Definitions Are Key in Debates over Theology," *World,* 28 February 1998, p. 21.

8. *Catechism of the Catholic Church* (Liguori, Mo.: Liguori, 1994), p. 371, pars. 1475–77.

9. Quoted in George et al., "An Open Letter," p. 9.

10. Edward E. Plowman, "Trent or Westminster?," *World,* 28 February 1998, p. 20.

11. Art Moore, "Does *The Gift of Salvation* Sell Out the Reformation?," *Christianity Today,* 27 April 1998, p. 17.

12. Michael P. Gendron, "*The Gift of Salvation:* Another Attempt at Compromise," *Proclaiming the Gospel Newsletter* (January 1998): 2, 3. This newsletter may be accessed at Proclaiming the Gospel Ministries' web site (http://www.pro-gospel.org/0198.html).

13. G. C. Berkouwer, *Vatikaans Concilie en Nieuwe Theologie* (Kampen: Kok, 1964), pp. 61–62. Cf. the English-language edition, *The Second Vatican Council and the New Catholicism,* trans. Lewis B. Smedes (Grand Rapids: Eerdmans, 1965), pp. 57–58: "Rome means to say by its notion of infallibility that the truth remains ever the same, lifted above the changes of history. . . . [Roman Catholics] are very aware that the life of the Church is not frozen into static sameness, . . . unaffected by the continuous process of growth and variation in history. History . . . has set its stamp on the Church. . . . We need only recall once again the condemnation of Galileo . . . [and] the gradual shifting of ground on the idea of natural evolution."

14. Hans Küng, *Kerk in Concilie* (Hilbersum: Paul Brand, 1963), pp. 148–49. See the English-language edition, *The Living Church: Reflections on the Second Vatican Council,* trans. Cecily Hastings and N. D. Smith (London: Sheed and Ward, 1963), pp. 306–7: ". . . *one* Faith can live in *different* formulas. One and the same good news is reported by four Evangelists in very different ways. . . . The Christian faith is historical in character and constantly formulates itself anew. . . . It was only in the fourth century that the attempt began to be made to establish one and the same formula throughout the Church. But the fundamental conviction remained that no one formula could suffice to account for the whole fullness of the Faith, and that difference in *formula* did not necessarily involve a difference in *faith.* Faith can be the same though formulas are not only different but . . . mutually opposed. Behind the different and contradictory formulations of faith stand different physiological, psychological, aesthetic, linguistic, logical, ethnological, historical, ideological, philosophical and religious presuppositions; different individual and collective experiences and languages and ideas about the world, different factors of environment and conceptions of man, different traditions held by individual nations, schools of theology, universities and religious orders." Italics his.

15. Küng, *Kerk in Concilie,* p. 149. See *The Living Church,* p. 307: "It often happened that all that was noticed in other people's statements was what was missing, while all that was noticed in one's own was what was there; that the *content* of truth in one's own formula and the *lack* of it in the other one were all that one took account of." Italics his.

16. James Buchanan, *The Doctrine of Justification: An Outline of Its History in the Church and of Its Exposition from Scripture* (1867; reprint, London: Banner of Truth, 1961), p. 131. Italics are Buchanan's.

17. Ibid., p. 134.

18. Ibid., p. 136.

19. Ibid.

20. Ibid., pp. 136–37.

21. Ibid., p. 137.

22. R. Scott Clark, "Regensburg and Regensburg II: Trying to Reconcile Irreconcilable Differences on Justification," *Modern Reformation* 7 (September 1998): 8. ARCIC is the Anglican–Roman Catholic International Commission, which issued in 1987 the statement *Salvation and the Church.*

Appendix 1, *The Gift of Salvation*

1. The first variant between the text of *The Gift of Salvation* as it appears in *Christianity Today* (8 December 1997, pp. 35–36, 38) and the text as it appears in *First Things* (Janu-

ary 1998, pp. 20–23) occurs here: “the Son” is “the Son,” in *First Things.* The version in appendix 1 is identical to that of *Christianity Today.*

2. “a knowledge” is “the knowledge” in *First Things.*

3. “5:9;” is “5:9,” in *First Things.*

4. “the gospel” is “the Gospel” in *First Things.* This variant is repeated in this paragraph and in paragraphs 15 and 19.

5. “God” is “God,” in *First Things.*

6. “half-hearted” is “halfhearted” in *First Things.*

7. “Evangelicals” is “Evangelical Protestants” in *First Things.*

8. “The Rev.” is “Rev.” in *First Things.*

9. “Dr. James I. Packer” is “Dr. James J. I. Packer” in *First Things.*

10. *First Things* also includes the following in its list of evangelical signees: Dr. Robert A. Seiple (World Vision U.S.).

11. “Fr.” is “Father” in *First Things* throughout its list of Roman Catholic signees.

12. “Emmanuel” is *“Emmanuel”* in *First Things.*

13. *First Things* also includes the following in its list of Roman Catholic signees: Mr. Keith Fournier (Catholic Alliance).

Appendix 2, *The Gospel of Jesus Christ*

1. Current as of May 19, 1999.

Glossary of Foreign Terms

The terms that follow are Latin unless otherwise identified. The abbreviation Gk. is for Greek.

ad hominem (form of argument in which one temporarily adopts the opponent's position in order to refute it), 151
Agnus Dei (Lamb of God), 138
alpha (Gk, first letter of alphabet), 30
anthropos (Gk, man), 134
a priori (from the former; deductively), 149
archē (Gk, beginning; chief, ruler), 131, 132
assensus (intellectual assent), 26, 27, 69, 168

beta (Gk, second letter of alphabet), 30

communio sanctorum (communion of the saints), 15
credo (I believe), 26

de facto (in fact, in reality), 39, 83
de jure (by right), 39
dicio (to speak), 33
didachē (Gk, teaching), 127, 176
dokein (Gk, to think, to seem or appear), 137
duplex iustitia (double imputation), 93

eis (Gk, into), 23
en (Gk, in), 23
e pluribus unum (from many, one), 25
esse (essence, being), 21
evangelium (Gk, gospel, good news), 33
ex opere operato (by the work performed), 71
extra nos (apart from us, outside of us), 65, 159

fides viva (vital, living faith), 69, 83–84
fiducia (personal trust; cognitive, affective, volitional faith), 26, 27, 69, 168, 169, 170, 171
fundamentum (foundation), 68

hagioi (Gk, saints, holy ones), 16
hic et nunc (here and now), 111
homoiousios (Gk, like or similar substance), 133–34
homoousios (Gk, same essence or substance), 133–34

initium (beginning), 68
iustitia acquisita (acquired righteousness), 93
iustitia inhaerens (inherent righteousness), 93
iustificare (to make just, justify, declare righteous), 71
iustitium alienum (alien righteousness), 65, 159

Index of Persons

Index of Scripture